Seeing Red
The politics of premenstrual tension

The Explorations in Feminism Collective

Jane Attala, Jane Cholmeley, Claire Duchen, Renate Duelli-Klein, Catherine Itzin, Diana Leonard, Pat Mahony, Caroline Waller

Explorations in Feminism

Close to Home
A materialist analysis of women's oppression
Christine Delphy
Edited and translated by Diana Leonard

Gender and Schooling
A study of sexual divisions in the classroom
Michelle Stanworth

Geography and Gender
An introduction to feminist geography
Women and Geography Study Group of the IBG

Going up into the Next Class
Women and elementary teacher training 1840–1914
Frances Widdowson

Helping Women at Work
The Women's Industrial Council, 1889–1914
Ellen Mappen

Man-Made Women
How new reproductive technologies affect women
G. Corca et al.

Schools for the Boys
Co-education reassessed
Pat Mahony

Seeing Red
The politics of premenstrual tension
Sophie Laws, Valerie Hey and Andrea Eagan

The Sexuality Papers
Male sexuality and the social control of women
Lal Coveney et al.

Well-Founded Fear
A community study of violence to women
Jalna Hanmer and Sheila Saunders

Seeing Red

The politics of premenstrual tension

Sophie Laws, Valerie Hey and Andrea Eagan

Introduction by Stevi Jackson

Hutchinson

London Melbourne Sydney Auckland Johannesburg

Hutchinson and Co. (Publishers) Ltd

An imprint of the Hutchinson Publishing Group

17–21 Conway Street, London W1P 6JD
and 51 Washington Street, Dover, New Hampshire 03820, USA

Hutchinson Publishing Group (Australia) Pty Ltd
16–22 Church Street, Hawthorn, Melbourne, Victoria 3122

Hutchinson Group (NZ) Ltd
32–34 View Road, PO Box 40–086, Glenfield, Auckland 10

Hutchinson Group (SA) (Pty) Ltd
PO Box 337, Bergvlei 2012, South Africa

First published 1985

Set in Times New Roman by Folio Photosetting, Bristol

Printed and bound in Great Britain by
Anchor Brendon Ltd,
Tiptree, Essex

British Library Cataloguing in Publication Data
Laws, Sophie
Seeing red: the politics of pre-menstrual tension.
— (Explorations in feminism; 9)
1. Premenstrual syndrome
I. Title II. Hey, Valerie III. Eagan, Andrea
IV. Series
618.1'72 RG165

Library of Congress Cataloging in Publication Data
Laws, Sophie.
Seeing red.

(Explorations in feminism)
Includes bibliographies.
1. Premenstrual syndrome — social aspects
2. Feminism. I. Hey, Valerie. II. Eagan, Andrea Boroff.
III. Title. IV. Series.
RG165.E24 1985 362.1'98175 85-14450

ISBN 0 09 160831 7

Contents

1 Introduction

Stevi Jackson

Women's feelings about premenstrual tension are often ambivalent. On the one hand, public discussion of it, and the fact that it has been recognized as a 'real' illness, might be welcomed as evidence of women's problems being taken seriously. On the other hand, many of us are wary of biologically based explanations of women's behaviour since they have so often been used to justify our subordination. We may fear that the idea of PMT has put another weapon into the hands of men who seek to discredit us, to make our demands on, or anger with them seem unreasonable, and now to deny the validity of our feelings by attributing them to 'the time of the month'. We may also suspect that the possibility of diagnosing PMT increases the power of the medical profession over our minds and bodies, enabling them to redefine real conflicts and tensions in our lives as sickness, and put pressure on us to conform.

These doubts are given expression and coherence by the articles in this book, which demonstrate how the concept of PMT can be and is used to discredit and control women. It becomes clear that PMT is not an isolated issue, but is linked to wider feminist concerns. It is of considerable relevance to debates on the social control of women; to the ways in which we are defined and categorized and our subordination legitimated and perpetuated.

There are a number of interrelated themes running through the book which are central to these debates. The authors take up the issue of biologistic explanations of sexual difference and the problems these pose for us regarding the way in which we perceive our own bodies. They relate this to the tendency for men to be defined as the biological norm against which women are judged to be deviant. They highlight the double standards applied to women's and men's behaviour and how the expectation that we will accommodate to men's needs and demands colours interpretations of our actions and our moods. These themes are brought together through analysing the construction of a PMT ideology which is profoundly misogynist in its assumptions and implications. This ideology is shown to operate at a variety of levels and through a variety of institutions. It is, moreover, having tangible effects on women's lives, from the invalidation of their anger and frustration to the prescription of potentially harmful drugs. It is manifested in our everyday dealings with men as well as in the doctor's surgery, the law courts and the media. It is enabling the pharmaceutical industry to increase its profits at women's expense.

In order to place the issue of PMT in context I will elaborate on the themes I have outlined. This will give some indication of the contribution this book makes to our growing knowledge of the continuities in, and endurance of, patriarchal ideologies.

I have suggested that one of the grounds for scepticism about PMT is that it lends itself to biologistic accounts of women's behaviour. It is a fundamental tenet of feminism that biology is not destiny. A great deal of feminist work has been devoted to revealing the flaws in the arguments and research which purport to prove that contemporary gender stereotypes reflect innate attributes of women and men, or that relations between women and men are dictated by the requirements of species survival. We have had to counter ever more sophisticated versions of biological determinism.

The authors of this book demonstrate that the ideology of PMT is indeed within this tradition. They present a thorough critique of the biologism it entails, exposing the sexist bias underlying the claims of PMT propagandists and the faults in the evidence they draw upon. The PMT syndrome emerges as having been constructed rather than 'discovered' by the medical profession. It is being used to discredit women, to explain both conformity to and deviance from 'normal' femininity.

It is also being used to justify treatment through hormone therapy. Both Sophie Laws and Andrea Eagan expose the dangers of taking progesterone to remedy a deficiency which has no proven existence. This raises serious questions about the vested interests of drug companies and PMT propagandists. As Andrea points out, feminists should have learnt by now to be wary of 'help' offered to women by the pharmaceutical industry.

One of the strengths of the arguments presented here is that they do not deny physical difference nor dismiss the effects of cyclical changes in women's bodies. Instead, they raise questions about how these are perceived within a patriarchal society; how these perceptions make it difficult for us to develop positive attitudes to the fact of our femaleness. Attempts to resist male definitions of our difference leave us suspended, as Valerie Hey says, between a 'bodiless politics' which denies difference and 'mother earth mysticism' which claims a mythical innate femaleness which patriarchy has distorted. To counteract the PMT ideology it is not necessary to refute the evidence of women's subjective experience of their cycles. We must, however, question the definitions and interpretations of that experience which have been imposed upon us.

The problem is not merely one of biologistic explanations of sexual difference, but lies also in the construction of the categories male and female. These are not symmetrical; they are neither equally weighted nor equally evaluated. Women are defined in relation *to* men as different *from* men. Men are taken as the norm, women the aberration; so that only men are regarded as truly representative of the human species. As Ros Coward has argued in relation to language, it is men who are permitted 'ungendered subjectivity', who can think of themselves simply as 'people'; women are always 'the sex', defined constantly by their gender (Coward and Black 1981). In the past this asymmetry was evident in religious legitimations of women's oppression: it was men, not women, who were made in God's image. Now it is reflected in scientific discourse where men are the model of the species against which women's bodies are assessed. It is decided in advance that any specifically female biological function is a peculiarity which needs to be explained. Hence cyclical change, being perceived as a purely female phenomenon, is itself regarded as suspect.

This is an aspect of what Betsy Ettorre has called the 'reproductive ideology' in which 'women appear falsely as more reproductive than men' (1980, p. 8). We are considered to be at the mercy of our reproductive biology whereas men are not. Women are frequently described as if we were no more than baby-making machines, whereas it is far rarer to find men referred to as nothing but mobile sperm banks. The hormones associated with our childbearing capacity are seen as far more problematic than 'male' hormones, and as far more likely to impel us into incomprehensible actions.

These assumptions underpin most scientific work on sexual difference, not merely that on PMT. Feminists have frequently pointed out that beneath the gloss of 'objectivity', scientific discourse is ideologically loaded. A pioneering exposé of the pretensions of patriarchal science is Ruth Herschberger's *Adam's Rib*, written in the 1940s. Of particular relevance to our understanding of PMT is her analysis of the assumptions about normality underlying a study of dominance in a pair of chimpanzees. It is of interest because it reveals the prejudices about cyclical change which shape perceptions of female behaviour.

Herschberger develops her critique by means of an imaginary interview in which Josie, the female chimpanzee in the study, gives her response to a report on the research written by one Professor Yerkes. He maintains that the male chimpanzee demonstrates his 'natural' dominance by taking possession of chunks of banana from the food chute except when the female is 'sexually receptive' when she claims the food even though she is the 'naturally subordinate member of the pair'. Josie contests this interpretation:

> Those words . . . look like somebody decided I was subordinate way in advance . . . any gains that I make when I'm sexually receptive can't be registered because the phase of maximal genital swelling is out of bounds . . . . If the period of sexual interest is, by implication, an extra natural phase in women (for it makes us *act* dominant when we're *naturally* subordinate), it looks like we girl chimps spend fourteen days out of twenty-four in the toils of Satan. (Herschberger 1970, pp. 8–9).

The ideology of PMT is rooted in the same assumptions and in the same style of reasoning. A phase of women's natural cycle is designated 'unnatural' so that any 'unfeminine' behaviour exhibited at that time is not 'normal' but the product of an 'abnormal' stage in the cycle. And what is 'normal' behaviour is decided for us, as with Josie, in advance. It is clear to Josie, too, that she is being defined in relation to the male chimp. She is described as sexually 'receptive' which, as she says, 'is one of those human words with an opinion written all over it' (ibid., p. 9). Her oestrous cycle is itself defined as abnormal because it interferes with her 'normal' female behaviour. She suggests that: 'Some woman scientist ought to start passing it around that males must be unnatural because they don't have cyclical changes during the month.' (ibid.)

Having defined cyclical change as abnormal and having arbitrarily classified parts of our cycles as being more abnormal than others, women's behaviour can be explained entirely by reference to our hormonal peculiarities. The press coverage of the Christine English trial described by Valerie Hey is a clear example of this. English's motives for killing her lover were reduced to her premenstrual state, and her grounds for feeling anger towards him ignored or discounted. With the increased publicity given to PMT, this form of biological reductionism is becoming commonplace. As Sophie Laws's chapter shows, men can attribute female behaviour or any problems in their relationships with women to 'the time of the month'.

PMT is an extremely flexible concept. It can be used to reinforce stereotypes of femininity as well as to explain 'unfeminine' conduct. It lends spurious scientific support to that well-worn sexist cliché, the unpredictable, irrational woman. It should be clear that this *is* a stereotype; there is no evidence that women are any less consistent or rational than men. There may well be a parallel here with the popular belief that women talk too much – whereas in fact, in mixed company, they talk a good deal less than men (Spender 1980).

A double standard is in operation here. Men's moods change, but this is not seen as requiring any explanation. Women's moods are seen as problematic because we are supposed to respond and accommodate to men's needs, not the other way around. The evidence Sophie Laws presents suggests that PMT is considered a problem not primarily because of the discomfort or distress it might cause women themselves, but because of its potentially disruptive effect on the lives of others, especially men (hence the emphasis placed on the responsibility of sufferers to seek treatment). A diagnosis of PMT exerts strong pressure on a woman to conform to others' wishes and expectations: any rebellious impulses are taken as symptomatic of her illness; any real problems in her life are interpreted as little more than delusions.

The norms to which women are expected to conform are not always consistent. We are expected to be feminine, but in order to be accepted in male-dominated spheres of public life we must conform to male codes of conduct, and become 'honorary men'. The only way in which any semblance of equality with men is achieved is by denying our femaleness. We are thus always potentially discreditable, the more so because of the selective perceptions and double standards by which we are judged. We must be careful lest anything we do or say reminds men of our difference and thus undermines our credibility.

Men's changes in mood or opinion can go unexplained. Women's are likely to be interpreted in terms of sexist stereotypes and are now increasingly frequently seen as signs of hormonal imbalance. It is hardly surprising, then, that PMT advice books stress the need for sufferers to ensure that their cyclical quirks do not impinge upon others. There is, however, another reason for this: the fear that PMT gives women an excuse for unacceptable or even criminal behaviour. This fear was evident in public responses to Christine English's trial.

The availability of such an excuse, however, is unlikely to benefit women in the long run. It is in keeping with the tendency to interpret women's crimes as psychiatric problems, to expose women deviants to 'treatment' rather than punishment, to incarcerate them in mental hospitals rather than prisons. Resorting to it is likely to rebound on us. If responsibility for our actions is denied in one context, it might lead to us being branded as irresponsible and unreliable in others. If PMT is accepted as a plausible legal defence, it could equally well be used to discredit women as witnesses. The potential consequences of this, especially in cases of violence against women, are extremely alarming.

This 'excuse', moreover, does not give women an unfair advantage in escaping the consequences of illegal and violent acts. It should hardly need to be pointed out that men who commit crimes of violence, especially when their victims are women, frequently avoid conviction and/or punishment by shifting the blame on to women via the notion of 'victim precipitation'. They do not need to plead that their hormones are out of balance.

There are two interrelated processes at play in the application of these double standards. First, there is the undermining of women's credibility whereby we are considered intrinsically less reliable than men. This process depends upon sexist stereotypes which were well established before the invention of PMT and into which the ideology of PMT fits very neatly. Second, there is the explanation of women's behaviour, rather than men's, in terms of biological functions.

Male biology may be used to explain general characteristics of masculinity, such as aggression and dominance, but it is only rarely used to account for the actions of individual men. While some forms of male criminality have been explained in biological terms, men in general are not thought to be governed by their bodies to the same degree as women. It is only women's hormones, not men's, which are held responsible for aberrant behaviour, since only women are considered to be at the mercy of their reproductive capacities. Again this mode of explanation existed prior to the invention of PMT and formed the context in which that invention took place. Our bodies have indeed, as Valerie Hey says, been 'long suspected'.

Read in the light of recent historical work on sexuality and women's oppression, this book shows PMT to be a legacy of a patriarchal heritage. It is part of an ideological tradition in which women have been, and continue to be, defined as the deviant category, as creatures peculiarly susceptible to the influence of their bodily functions.

This is particularly well documented from the nineteenth century onwards, when science supplanted religion as the main set of discourses through which women's subordination was legitimated. Where women were once suspected as potential witches, their bodies regarded as impure, their unreliability attributed to the 'fall', men's suspicions of women were translated into scientific terms. Reproductive biology has since been used to explain not only that form of deviance from the male norm called 'femininity', but also to account for deviance from femininity itself, or indeed any form of deviant behaviour in women.

It was also in the nineteenth century that gynaecological disorders came to be more frequently and more systematically associated with 'abnormal' sexual desires and practices, with mental illness and with criminal behaviour (Foucault 1979; Edwards 1981). Medical technology has become more sophisticated, models of femininity have become increasingly sexualized, but the basic contours of the discourses through which these associations are made have changed little. Doctors no longer diagnose hysteria but hormonal imbalance. They prescribe doses of progestogens rather than clitoridectomy. The existence of sexual desire in women no longer makes them suspect some gynaecological malfunction. Instead, in an age when women are expected to be continuously available to their male partners, it is lack of libido which is cause for concern.

The associative link between reproduction, sexuality and deviance is still a major means of defining and categorizing women. It has been noted, for example, in the 'sexualization' of female delinquency, whereby attention is shifted from the original delinquent act to girls' sexual behaviour or their deviance explained by some imputed sexual problem (Smart 1976). It is the means by which PMT can be made to explain any aspect of women's behaviour, can be cited as precipitating unusual criminal acts yet is claimed to be so common as to be part of the normal female condition.

The idea that the menstrual cycle is both the origin of pathology and pathological in itself also dates from the nineteenth century. All manner of theorists from eminent gynaecologists to the sociologist Emile Durkheim concurred with this view (Edwards 1981). Menstruation was believed to be responsible for hysteria, delusions and mental derangement. The analysis may now be more subtle, the terminology more obscure, but the basic argument remains. It may be the premenstrual phase rather than menstruation itself which is seen as particularly problematic, but women are still believed to be governed by their menstrual cycles and thus given to bizarre unpredictable behaviour.

In analysing a modern product of this long patriarchal tradition, neither Valerie Hey nor Sophie Laws seek to deny women's subjective experience of their menstrual cycles. Instead they concentrate on how they have been defined, and how we are encouraged to define them ourselves, in negative, damaging terms. The invention of PMT does not mean that women's problems are being taken more seriously, but that our credibility is being undermined and our experience invalidated. It is not a means of promoting more understanding attitudes towards women, but of getting us to conform. It is not about the relief of suffering, but about suppressing the pain of women's lives, blocking its expression and preventing its material causes being confronted. The arguments mustered here demonstrate convincingly and forcefully that, understood in the context of a patriarchal social order, PMT is yet another ideological weapon used to define and control women.

References

Ros Coward and Maria Black, 'Linguistic, social and sexual relations: a review of Dale Spender's "Man-Made Language", *Screen Education*, no. 5 (1981).

Susan Edwards, *Female Sexuality and the Law* (Martin Robertson, Oxford 1981).

Betsy Ettore, *Lesbians, Women and Society* (Routledge & Kegan Paul, London, 1980).

Michel Foucault, *The History of Sexuality*, vol. 1 (Penguin, Harmondsworth, 1979).

Ruth Herschberger, *Adam's Rib* (Harper and Row 1970).

Carol Smart, *Women, Crime and Criminology: A feminist critique* (Routledge & Kegan Paul, 1976).

Dale Spender, *Man-Made Language* (Routledge & Kegan Paul, 1980).

2 Who needs PMT?
A feminist approach to the politics of premenstrual tension*

Sophie Laws

Preface

PMT has made me nervous for some time. As a women's health worker, other women used often to ask me what I thought about it, and I never knew what to say. As a feminist, I try to understand my life in new ways, refusing to accept male-centred ways of thinking which deny or distort my own experience. I find I have contradictory and confusing feelings about the menstrual cycle, and there seems to be little feminist work to look to. In 1981 I began a research project on the social aspects of menstruation. Almost as soon as I had begun that work, two cases came to court where women were offering PMT as a defence against criminal charges. This forced me to think again about PMT.

The press coverage of those cases, which Valerie Hey discusses in her chapter, shocked me and led me to read further – I turned first to the popular advice books, as they appeared to be offering a more feminist view. I was appalled at the ideas about women I actually found there. I tried to compare their assertions to what the medical and scientific 'experts' say. And I talked with other women about what I found there.

This chapter is my attempt to make sense of what is said about PMT from a radical feminist point of view.

---

* Writing this article was made possible for me by the interest and encouragement of a great many women. My thanks especially to Lynn Alderson, Katy Gardner, Judy Greenway, Hilary Homans, Sandra McNeill, Lisa Saffron and Margaret Stacey, who gave me essential criticism and support.

Introduction

As one man told me: 'I thought there was something mentally wrong with my wife. And I think she even thought she was a bit unstable. But when we realised the connection with her periods it suddenly all made sense!' (Judy Lever, *PMT, the unrecognised illness*)

It is estimated that from 25 to 100 per cent of women suffer from some form of pre-menstrual emotional disturbance.... Eicher makes the discerning point that the few women who do not admit to premenstrual tension are basically unaware of it, but one needs only to talk to their husbands, or co-workers, to confirm its existence. (Richard I. Shader and Jane I. Ohly, *Pre-menstrual Tension, Femininity and Sexual Drive*)

Hence, there is no natural (wild) state of femaleness that is legitimated/allowed in the Gynecological State, and this denial of female be-ing is the essence of its gynocidal intent. There are only two possibilities. First there is a fallen state, formerly named sinful and symbolised by Eve, presently known as sick and typified in the powerless but sometimes difficult and problematic patient. Second, there is the restored/redeemed state of perfect femininity, formerly named saintly and symbolised by Mary, presently typified in the weak, 'normal' women whose normality is so elusive that it must constantly be re-enforced through regular check-ups, 'preventive medicine' and perpetual therapy. (Mary Daly, *Gyn/Ecology*)

Over the last few years there has been a good deal of debate about premenstrual tension in this country, and not just within the medical profession. It has often been said that this public discussion is good for women, breaking down a taboo, bringing us medical help. At last, women's problems are being taken seriously by doctors. But are they? Does the medical definition of PMT* actually describe correctly what women are feeling?

---

* Some doctors have recently taken to using the term 'premenstrual syndrome' (PMS) instead of premenstrual tension, claiming that this is a more accurate scientific term. When something gets a bad name, one tactic is to change the name rather than the thing – Long Kesh, the prison in Northern Ireland, becomes The Maze; Windscale, the nuclear power station in Cumbria, becomes Sellafield. I prefer to use the term premenstrual tension because it is the one most people recognize.

There tend to be two sides to the argument. Either women aren't really much affected by their menstrual cycles and just use them as excuses for bad behaviour; or some, perhaps most, menstruating women suffer a time of illness each month during which time they are not responsible for their actions. Both these views are anti-woman. We need not accept that these are the only choices we have.

So how can we understand the ways in which our menstrual cycles affect our lives? I suggest that we must begin by looking carefully at what we are being offered as a description of our experiences, and at where it comes from. We must begin to see this as a *political* issue.

We must ask in whose interests is it that PMT is becoming accepted as a medical condition? Have its promoters really discovered new truths about female biology? What evidence is there that hormones can *control* human behaviour in the way that is claimed? How does the idea of PMT encourage us to see women in general? Should we necessarily see cyclic change as in itself a bad thing? And are the 'symptoms' of PMT signs of sickness or could they be reasonable reactions to the world?

In this chapter I am not proposing new 'truths' about women's experience of their menstrual cycles. All I am hoping to do here is undertake a work of critique: to lay bare a piece of male ideology and to challenge the 'scientific' evidence used to support it.

Politics and women's bodies

Feminists have always recognized the political importance of the health and control of women's bodies. However it is not always at all obvious which approaches to women's health will turn out to be most positive for women. There seems to be a deep conflict between the need for us to control our bodies, especially our fertility, and the need of our bodies to be left alone. While we remain in many ways dependent on the medical profession and bound by existing medical knowledge it is extremely difficult to work out where our control of our bodies ends, and their control of us begins. Many of us have found ourselves longing for freedom from our bodies (an aspiration which is encouraged by the male view of women as defective men), and unable to conceive of women becoming free *in* our bodies.

Debates over a 'woman's place' have frequently centred on the female body, and, particularly in the nineteenth century, anti-feminist rhetoric has leaned heavily on the notion that women are physically inferior to men. Women's childbearing ability has been used *ad nauseam* to claim that women's bodies are also specially designed for floor scrubbing, cooking, washing, etc., in the service of men. In the 1960s the Pill was offered as a chance of 'liberation' for women: thus women's bodies, and the possibility of pregnancy, were blamed for women's oppression. Men benefit from and perpetuate women's oppression, but this has been concealed by blaming misfortunes which actually result from male domination on to women's bodies. So what is actually a social phenomenon, male domination, appears to result from female weakness. For many of us the ability of our bodies to become pregnant has seemed to us to be our point of vulnerability, from which contraception would protect us. This history, among other things, has left us a legacy of mistrust of our bodies.

Liberal feminism has been based in part on the hope that women might be accepted by men into their world if we can bring our bodies under strict control; if we can ensure that our femaleness is not apparent to them in any offensive fashion.

This could never work in the long run: women cannot be sneaked, in disguise, into the bastions of male power! Women who attempt to enter the world of men on this basis are terrorized by men's insistence on an appearance of sanitized femininity, and punished by sexual harassment. Silvia Rodgers (1981) describes how the British House of Commons operates as a 'men's house', where women members have to be reclassified as honorary men. Life is made very difficult, therefore, for a woman MP who is pregnant or breastfeeding, for her femaleness becomes too visible. Women MPs are also routinely subjected to sexual jokes and jeers which are quite unlike the relatively gentle joking which goes on between the men.

In recent years men seem to have taken to using PMT as a weapon for putting women in their place. A woman who expresses anger or admits to feeling under stress will often be asked, pityingly or aggressively, if it is 'that' time of the month.

PMT is only one of the many ways in which women's learnt hatred of their bodies is expressed: others are slimming, self-starvation, obsession with appearance, plastic surgery including breast surgery . . . the list goes on and on. I feel that for women to act in the world on their own behalf, we need also to free ourselves from the undermining effects of this body-hatred. Women are debilitated, it is true, by more than their fair share of actual ill health, but it is also debilitating for a human being to live in constant doubt as to whether or not she is 'normal'. It seems to me that women are being encouraged to search themselves regularly, rather as police search suspects, for signs of wrongness, disease. The new attention to 'women's health' will certainly have backfired on us if it turns out to mean that women have to be more rather than less worried about their health.

The menstrual cycle has now been transformed by the medical profession into something only experts can tell us about. Women are supposed to be at the mercy of it, and our hopes for release depend upon doctors gaining a full understanding and finally control of it. The medical description of the menstrual cycle is taught to women, rather than women's own versions of their experiences being listened to: if you deviate from their norm, you need treatment. PMT is part of this medical model, not an idea which came from women.

PMT is not only an imposed category. It provides a survival strategy for women. If unacceptable parts of one's personality can be labelled PMT and regarded as the results of a pitiable hormonal imbalance, one can retain one's hold on a self-definition as a good woman. Now, at the societal level, PMT may become a possible legal defence. Some women I spoke to about these cases said 'Oh, great, next time I get into trouble I'll make sure I'm premenstrual.' From the judge's point of view, then, they need not believe that *women* are ever violent, aggressive, anti-social but that women with PMT are. And women can use this to deny responsibility for their actions. This may be necessary or even useful in dealing with an unjust legal system, but the wider consequences are alarming.

Women divided

Dividing women from women and a woman against herself are important functions of patriarchal ideology. As the quotation from Mary Daly at the start of this chapter indicates, it is central to the male view of women that there are Good women and Bad women.

Children are taught about Cinderella and the Ugly Sisters, Snow White and her wicked stepmother. Good women in real life are generally defined by having or at least desiring an acceptable relationship with a man: faithful wife, virginal daughter, kindly mother. Bad women are equally stereotyped: whore, frigid wife, nymphomaniac, lesbian, nagging mother-in-law, old witch. You know the kind of thing.

The problem with the 'bad' category is that if many actual women were acknowledged to occupy it, this would imply that a certain amount of rebellion existed among women. Instead, however, the formulation tends to be that women are all saintly underneath but that for various reasons some of them become ill and exhibit irrational or bad behaviour at times as a result of their illness. PMT isolates the badness in women to a part of themselves which is only sometimes there and which results from influences (hormones) beyond their control. Some quotations to illustrate this:

> Jane, a journalist, found this problem: '... usually I'm very even-tempered but in these times it is as if someone else, not me, is doing all this and it is very frightening.' (Lever 1980, p. 35)

> Many women describe themselves as 'A sort of Jekyll and Hyde', most of the time capable, loving and able to cope and then suddenly quite the reverse. (ibid, p. 39)

> I am witchy as hell just before the flow starts. (Weideger 1978, p. 50)

> ... sudden mood changes, irrational behaviour, and bursting into tears for no apparent reason are bewildering (to a husband), while sudden aggression and violence are deeply disturbing when with little warning and no justification, his darling little love bird suddenly becomes an angry, argumentative, shouting, abusive bitch. (Dalton 1978)

Notice the repetition of the word 'sudden', emphasizing the idea of a sharp interruption of normal life. Brush, too, describes his typical patient as complaining 'I feel as if I'm turning into another person.' (Brush 1977, p. 12).

Katharina Dalton and other PMT doctors have received a lot of favourable publicity as champions of womankind – yet it seems to me that what they actually defend is the ideal of the traditionally feminine women. They use statistics to blame women for a most extraordinary range of acts of disruption and violence. Judy Lever's book, for example, contains allegations that PMT causes increased criminal offences, baby battering and accidents to children, attacks on husbands, suicide attempts, heavy drinking, accidents in the home, at work, on the road, broken marriages – even wife battering: 'his wife provokes him by her own violent behviour when suffering from PMT' (Lever 1980, p. 69). This is a fairly standard list for the PMT literature, though items drop in and out of it between different authors. For instance, although a lessened interest in sex is sometimes included in the symptom list, Dalton wrote recently that:

> Among PMS women, increased libido is occasionally noticed in the premenstruum, a fact recorded by Israel back in 1938. All too often it is this nymphomaniac urge in adolescents which is responsible for young girls running away from home, or custody, only to be found wandering in the park or following the boys. These girls can be helped, and their criminal career abruptly ended with hormone therapy. (Dalton 1982a)

Yet the doctors maintain at the same time that women are innocent, misunderstood victims of their hormones. PMT patients want to be *nice*:

> Then suddenly her irritability ends. She is once more her usual sweet tempered and placid self, or she may be filled with guilt and remorse at the problems her actions have caused. One woman said 'I wish others would realize that it wasn't the true me who caused all this'. (Dalton 1969, p. 62)
>
> Another pleads 'If only you could give me something so that I'm not so spiteful against my fiancé, whom I really do love'. (ibid, p. 111)

The advertisement used in medical journals for Cyclogest (progesterone pessaries) also illustrates with plodding clarity this imagery of Good woman vs. Bad woman. The photograph shows two versions of one woman: one in a black round-necked tee shirt with untidy hair and a sad expression, the second with shining hair, a shining smile and a white V-neck blouse.

PMT can be used to completely invalidate a woman's feelings. Dalton cites with sympathy a marriage guidance counsellor who 'arranges to see both partners eight days after they quarrel: in this way he hopes that the woman will have safely passed through both her premenstruum and her menstruation before the time of the interview' (ibid, p. 112). This man then simply refuses to contemplate women's feelings at this time – he declares them invalid and places them outside the range of what must be dealt with in repairing the marital relationship.

I think that many women will recognize this situation, where a man feels that he can ignore what you say if you are premenstrual at the time you say it. A man who is spoken to angrily by a woman can at any time quietly comfort himself with the idea that she's only upset because of her hormones. PMT, of course, only covers women who menstruate: anger in older women can be put down to the menopause, in pregnant women to their state of pregnancy, in adolescent women to their adolescence, in women who don't have period or whose periods are irregular to their hormonal peculiarity. It's a pretty complete system, and each part of it supports all the others!

Miriam Stoppard would like us to do the undermining for ourselves: 'You may even confess during the bad times that you know you are behaving improperly. If not, admit to your loss of control when you feel well again' (Stoppard 1982). According to Dalton, men are well pleased with her treatments: 'Many a husband has commented after the first course of injections that his wife is now more like the woman he knew at their marriage' (Dalton 1969, p. 73). How pleasant to be able to attribute any problem in a marriage to the wife's illness! The husband need not even consider whether there could be any *other* reasons why his wife might have changed since they married.

Lack of acceptance of one's 'dangerous' side goes deep in all human beings, perhaps, but it is especially taught to women. A woman I worked with once described a period of the time we worked together: 'Oh yes, that was the time you were premenstrual most of the time.' I had been putting my crossness, tension and exhaustion down to PMT in what was apparently an obviously unrealistic way. It would have been much more disturbing for me and for us all to look at why I was in such a state, and to admit that it was something we might be able to change.

That women are being turned against one another is perhaps also reflected in feminists' responses to the idea of PMT. PMT can appear as a kind of defence of womankind against the charge of being moody and unpredictable, as it isolates the change to a specific time period and names it an illness. It can then, for instance, be argued that women in general are fit to do 'men's work', so long as it is understood that *some* women have PMT and special allowances must be made for them at 'those' times. So women may disown and pity either other women or parts of themselves while maintaining a basic view of 'women' as reasonable, consistent, acceptable human beings – just like men.

Female complaints

Gynaecological practice can be seen as a continuous tradition of activity at the front line of the struggle between men and women. PMT should be seen as part of that tradition, not as a new liberatory concept which breaks with it. The theory of female physiology which gynaecologists have produced is rooted in and consists of their own practice, which has been a history of disaster for women. PMT springs from that theory.

Reading modern writings about PMT, I was strongly reminded of discussions among feminist historians about the 'female complaints' from which nineteenth-century women were said to suffer. In the second half of the nineteenth century in Britain and the USA there was great public concern about invalidism among middle- and upper-class women. It is difficult for us to know what those women were experiencing. The medical descriptions are often very clearly descriptions of a rebellious woman. All women's thoughts and deeds tended to be put down to something wrong with their reproductive organs. Dr Isaac Ray wrote in the 1860s that all women should be seen as hovering on the verge of hysteria, insanity and crime:

> With women it is but a step from extreme nervous susceptibility to downright hysteria, and from that to overt insanity. In the sexual evolution, in pregnancy, in the parturient period, in lactation, strange thoughts, extraordinary feelings, unseasonable appetites, criminal impulses, may haunt a mind at other times innocent and pure.

Besides these dangers of the normal female body, any gynaecological disorder was widely thought to lead to insanity.

There has been a good deal of debate among feminists as to how this phenomenon should be interpreted. Were the women 'really ill'? Were they using illness to express rebellion? Was the language of illness used by the medical men as a technique for controlling women? (Hartman and Banner 1974; Ehrenreich and English 1979). The public debate in that period ran along the same lines as the present one about PMT – are women lying, or are they terribly sick?

What we do know is what was done to women who were said to be suffering from hysteria, nymphomania, or whatever it was. Treatment with electricity – electrodes introduced into the uterus – was widely practised; ovaries were cut out; the clitoris was cut out; sometimes the womb itself was removed (Daly 1978, Barker-Benfield 1975). 'Local massage', which sounds very like a kind of sexual assault, was very common. Leeches were applied to the perineum and to the cervix. Women were slapped around the face and neck with wet towels. Drugs were given, some of them poisonous ones (Edwards 1981). And then there was the Wier-Mitchell 'rest cure' which involved the woman being isolated in bed, denied any mental stimulation, seeing only the doctor and a nurse, and being overfed and massaged daily. The idea, explicitly stated, was that she should be reduced to total dependency, and that she should learn to accept that male authority was good for her.

Medicine in general in that period tended to go in for techniques which seem to us barbaric in the extreme. What is striking about what was done to women is that the doctors often stated quite openly their intention to bring them under their control. One doctor describes women suffering from 'simple hysterical mania' like this:

> They rapidly become less and less conventional. Thus a lady will smoke, talk slang, or be extravagant in dress; and will declare her intention of doing as she likes. At this stage love affairs, and the like complications are common. (in Allbutt 1899, p. 355)

It is also notable that all this went on in the period when the first wave of modern feminism was taking shape. Charlotte Perkins Gilman, an American feminist writer, was subjected to the rest cure, and wrote *The Yellow Wallpaper*, a powerful, subtle, polemic against such treatment of women (Gilman 1981).

It is interesting, too that, as with the ladylike stereotype of the nineteenth-century female invalid, PMT sufferers are often said by doctors to be predominantly middle class. Garrey *et al.*, for example, say that:

Marriage and childbirth do not affect PMT but there is usually a preponderance of the more articulate patients, especially professional women who appear before the public and cannot easily stay off work. (Garrey *et al.* 1978, p. 120)

This assertion that PMT has a class basis often reads like a roundabout way of saying that the more downtrodden women are, the happier they are.

I am not claiming that the modern enthusiasm for PMT is exactly parallel to these female complaints of the nineteenth century. But there are certain similarities. In the same way, all women are suspected of being ill and will be accused of harbouring a hidden sickness if they step out of line. Also female behaviour is attributed to the state of their reproductive system – the hormones presently under suspicion are produced by and act on the ovaries, which were an important target of surgery in the nineteenth century. Indeed Frank, when he first coined the term premenstrual tension, discussed both oophorectomy (the removal of the ovaries) and sterilization by X-ray as possible cures, as late as 1931.

Let me make it clear that I am not suggesting, as others have done, that unhappy women through the ages have 'really' had PMT! What we are seeing is two roughly similar movements by which medical 'science' is used to conceal female oppression and rebellion, and to undermine women's self-respect – the precise mechanisms are not the same.

PMT as an idea is not by any means yet fully accepted by the medical establishment – many doctors still tend to the view that women are making it up. Therefore it appears as an evangelical movement, claiming to be on women's side. In the next section I look at the ideological content of the literature which promotes PMT.

PMT industry anti-woman

The PMT advice books written for the popular market, put their position very clearly, and form the most straightforward statement of the PMT ideology of the last few years. These are not, of course, 'pure' sources, in the sense that they do not try to make consistent arguments, and often give no evidence at all for the statements they make. The newspaper articles may, for all I know, misquote their interviewees. The point is that this is where most women will derive their impressions about what PMT is supposed to be. These kinds of writings have an influence which is to some degree independent of the scientific 'proofs' they use to back themselves up.

Each of the three books I have looked at in detail has an introductory statement from a man, sanctioning them with remarks about the importance of the topic. The two written by lay women, Beryl Kingston's *Lifting the Curse* and Judy Lever's *PMT: the unrecognised illness*, have prefaces by male doctors, and Dr Katharina Dalton's book *The Menstrual Cycle* is introduced by her 'husband and ghost-writer', the Rev. Tom E. Dalton. His statement is particularly clear, so I will quote at length:

> These findings she has set down in this book so that all who read it may understand the extent to which the cyclical changes in the levels of a woman's hormones are responsible for her unpredictable changes of personality. The reader will begin to realise that there is a biological basis for much that has been written, or said, about the whims and vagaries of women. The old cliché 'It's a woman's privilege to change her mind' calls for even greater tolerance than before now that it is realised that every woman is at the mercy of the constantly recurring ebb and flow of her hormones. (Dalton 1969, p. 7)

These books put forward a most alarming list of dreadful things women do during the premenstrual phase. From the panicky tone of the writing, one would think that violent crime committed by women was *the* social problem of our times. And yet when we look at the figures for offenders found guilty of the kinds of offences the PMT books talk about – murder, manslaughter, infanticide, other violence against the person, sexual offences and criminal damage – the picture is rather different. In 1982, of the 81,000 found guilty of these crimes, only 6700 were women. Among these women, the most common offence was 'violence against the person' short of killing – but there were still nine times more men than women in this category (*Social Trends* 1984). And of course we know too that the vast majority of acts of violence to women by men – wife-battering and rape – never even come to court, as they are regarded as private, domestic matters.

Books like these tend to simplify in blinding ways. Each gives some descriptions of menstrual taboos and restrictions, which are listed all together and described as belonging to some past time or to uncivilized societies. Then 'science' is invoked to explain these supposedly incomprehensible things:

> In those days people thought there was something magic or evil about menstrual blood. Now we know that it's chemistry that's doing the damage. We're clumsy and accident-prone because the chemical balance of our bodies is upset. (Kingston 1980, p. 63)

Men's ways of dealing with menstruation in different cultures are run together with women's premenstrual experience in our own – and 'chemistry' is blamed. Other explanations, based on social or political factors such as the power relations between men and women, are brushed aside, and people are seen as reacting in an automatic way to women's universally disturbed hormones.

Understatement is an important technique which they use to sidestep difficult issues – a hearty tone must be maintained at all times. Judy Lever, for instance, gives a pretty devastating list of the elaborate restrictions on menstruating women enforced by all the 'world' religions and suggests, finally, that this 'reinforces the feeling that there is something not quite "nice" about menstruation' (pp. 59–60). There is an implication that women would 'naturally' feel all this anyway. The very intense messages, backed with threats, which patriarchal cultures deliver to women about how they should feel about menstruation, are reduced to some slight feeling of impropriety – a feeling which the woman could presumably be expected to overcome quite easily if she is not neurotic?

There are contradictions, though – the authors sometimes express some indignation about the way women are treated, and generally give a nod to the idea that social factors increase women's sufferings. But anything of this kind is far outweighed by the space given to therapy, all kinds of which naturally focus on the individual. Beryl Kingston does include a section on what she calls pressure group tactics, ways to push employers and schools to take menstrual problems into consideration, but she ends it: 'Last but not least, try not to look too fierce! A smile gets results much quicker than a snarl' (p. 89).

A Birmingham gynaecologist who runs a PMT clinic has no such problems about a woman's place. He advocates the use of a drug still in the experimental stage which stops the cycle altogether:

> 'Some women are disturbed by not having periods, they think it is unnatural,' says Dr Parsons. 'But if you are talking about what Mother Nature intended, it is for a woman to get pregnant with her first period and spend the rest of her life bearing children until she dies at 40. PMT is unnatural, so is the menopause.' (Sarah Pepper, *Coventry Evening Telegraph*, 4 May 1982)

This is quite a common medical attitude towards PMT. The fantasy of the 'natural woman' it relies upon is most alarming. Why *should* we imagine hunger (leading to early death) and enforced sex (leading to constant pregnancy) to be what 'Mother Nature' intended for women?

A booklet from Women's Health Care also follows this line of thinking, that 'modern' women suffer especially because they may have jobs as well as 'looking after homes and families', without the 'help once available . . . the extended family and the close-knit community'. How this affects one's hormones is unclear. But no need to worry, dear, if you're being worked to death – there's a pill for it:

> This is one of the disadvantages of modern living, and to compensate women need whatever advantages are available. Fortunately these include today better and more effective medical treatments.

These are, of course, guidebooks to survival in a man's world – Kingston's book, particularly, goes in for rather obvious solutions to the difficulties of everyday life. There is a section on relaxing standing up*, and a lot of helpful remarks like 'It's difficult to be decent *and* relax your legs and thighs' and 'Make all your decisions in the week you're not depressed' (pp. 25, 65).

If women are to act in the world of men, they must fit themselves to the male norm. Dalton remarks that some firms have started to

---

* You want to know how it's done? Mostly you sit down whenever you can.

have what she describes as 'luxurious rest rooms' for their female employees. She disapproves. A better approach, she suggests, would be to fix up those few awkward women who have failed to fix themselves:

> one wishes that instead their industrial medical advisors would sift out those employees to whom a new lease of life could be given by the correct administration of hormone therapy and arrange for them to receive treatment. (Dalton 1964)

The largest section of each book deals with a great range of treatments to relieve menstrual problems including PMT. Relaxation techniques and breathing control as practised in 'natural' childbirth classes are especially advocated by Erna Wright (1975) and Beryl Kingston, and often crop up in passing elsewhere. Kingston writes of 'nervous tension', that state where a woman is full of energy and rushes about doing things, wanting to work at all hours, that this 'symptom' particularly upsets husbands. She therefore advises women in this state to lie down for at least half an hour and practice their relaxation techniques. She concedes that one woman told her that this just made her worse, but is none the less completely locked into the assumption that it is the woman who is 'out of tune' (p. 64).

Sir Norman Jeffcoate, in his *Principles of Gynaecology* (1975), also advocates rest. He suggests that 'A sleep of two hours in the middle of every day is particularly helpful' as part of the 'reorganisation of her life or her outlook on life (which) is often necessary' (p. 547). A sleep in the afternoon might be very pleasant for anyone, including a busy gynaecologist, after a hard morning in survery - but somehow it is not suggested as an answer to men's problems. Women, of course, can be assumed to have nothing of any importance to do with their days.

How to spot the 'genuine sufferer'

Though at first the PMT propagandists were happy to encourage as many women as possible to identify PMT in themselves, some of them now seem to be concerned to distinguish 'real' PMT sufferers from other women. They could not fail to notice that the press and the public were not making this distinction in the debate after the court cases involving PMT, and all women were being accused of suffering PMT. Or was it more worrying to them that many women apparently began to offer PMT as an 'excuse' for numerous crimes?

Whatever the reasons, doctors have been reported to be anxious about this – a few months after her courtroom successes, Dalton was taking on quite a threatening tone towards women. In an interview with Sarah Crompton in the *Coventry Evening Telegraph* (15 July 1982), she is quoted as follows:

In general she believes women must not use PMS as an excuse. If they suffer from it – mildly or severely – there is treatment and they should take it. She says 'I think women have a duty if they know they are going to break something and going to be irritable to be treated and to look after themselves. They owe it to themselves and to women in general. Otherwise they will get what they deserve from men.'

But how *is* the true sufferer to be identified? In an article in *World Medicine*, Dalton stresses doctors' duty to ensure that the plea of PMT should not be abused: 'in every case the diagnosis of PMS (should be) substantiated with incontrovertible evidence and that it will respond to treatment. Only the doctor can provide such evidence....' A woman, she says, must be able to show that she has a history of 'recurrent symptoms' – and in establishing this, everyone's word will be taken seriously but her own: 'Such evidence might be supplied by her employers, friends or family, or by searching through diaries, medical files, police records or prison documents.' To illustrate what she means, she mentions that

Incidentally, each of the three women reported in *The Lancet* was referred for diagnosis of PMS by her father, who had noticed his daughter's unpredictable behaviour occurred every four weeks. The three offenders had pain-free menstruation and had not themselves associated this cyclic physiologial event with their strange behaviour. (1982b)

The essence of the doctor's expertise, here, seems to be that they know who is to be believed. Daddy knows best.

As we have seen, Dalton is now also advocating the idea that the true sufferer can be identified by her willingness to accept treatment, and by her condition being improved when treated. Dalton is now reported as suggesting that there are only a few 'genuine sufferers' among women charged with criminal offences, though her own statistics (Dalton 1961) are often quoted as showing that a large proportion of women who are convicted of crimes committed them during their premenstrual period (Sarah Crompton, *Coventry Evening Telegraph*, 15 July 1982).

One of the most obvious differences between nineteenth-century doctors' statements and the PMT industry's is that in the nineteenth century doctors quite openly gave forth moral judgements. Since then, increasingly, the language of health has replaced that of morality, so that women who fail to marry, or who fail to be happy when married, lesbians, and other deviants, are seen as probably ill rather than probably evil. The 'healthy' woman is calm, contented, well-adjusted, able to cope. An unhappy woman is encouraged to think about her diet, whether she is getting enough exercise, and the state of her hormones, before she may consider that her life may be making her unhappy. The PMT promoters can hide their prescriptions for female behaviour behind medical rhetoric.

PMT must be seen in the context of the punitive way in which female suffering in general is treated. In particular we can see similarities with the treatment of women said to be 'mentally ill'. In that case, also, the choice is offered between pulling yourself together and taking stupefying drugs. In both cases, women's pain is to be suppressed, not expressed, and what such women say is not taken seriously.

The PMT industry is campaigning for more women to be put into the 'sick' category. Dalton's remark that if women refuse to get treatment, to control themselves chemically, they will get what they deserve from men, reveals clearly that PMT is about getting women to conform and not about changing the world to make women's lives more bearable.

'The unrecognized illness'?

Since the recent publicity about PMT, women have been going to doctors in large numbers complaining of it. Much of the thrust of the pro-PMT lobby's argument is that women *want* it to be defined as a medical problem. All the doctors who are studying PMT refer to huge responses from women whenever they appear in the media discussing it. They take this as evidence that it is a real medical problem 'out there'.

It is clear that women want acceptance of the reality of the cyclic change they know they experience; but need we accept that PMT as a 'syndrome' exists because of this? Clearly what is called PMT refers to real experiences. What we must bring into question is the whole category – how we are being taught to describe cyclic changes we notice, and *why*: who benefits from this kind of description? It is difficult to think beyond the categories we are accustomed to using. Let me explain why I think we should make the effort: why I believe that it is possible for us to rethink PMT.

Most of the time, if someone came round asking us in detail about our health, most of us would have something or other we could complain to them about. Surveys have found that at any given time up to 90 per cent of the adult population is aware of the presence of some symptom which, if it was taken to a doctor, would be considered 'clinically serious' (e.g. Pearse and Crocker 1949; Siegel 1963). Thus a state of illness, in one sense, appears to be statistically the norm. And yet most of the time we don't see ourselves as ill.

'Being ill', then, is a social process, which we may or may not decide to enter into when we experience some feeling which could be called a symptom. The actions which follow from (or, rather, constitute) a decision to 'be ill' – stopping work, going to the doctor, and so on – clearly do not follow automatically from feeling a pain, or suspecting some bodily malfunction.

So one must examine not why people who have symptoms do not take any action but rather why some people do, and why they do so at the time that they do. I. K. Zola undertook a study exploring this question in 1966, looking at people attending the outpatients clinic of the General Eye and Ear Hospital in Boston, Massachusetts (see also Zola 1973). What is interesting about this survey, for our purposes here, is that it focused on complaints which medical science places in an entirely 'physical' category – these people could be diagnosed as having good solid identifiable illnesses. While the medical profession certainly believes that people present them with complaints which they cannot categorize tidily at times which are arbitrary or which relate more to their social lives than to their physical condition, this study shows that this in fact applies to all kinds of illness. To say that because of some social event in her life a person decides that some problem with her vision, for instance, is an illness requiring treatment, is not to say that she does not have a problem with her sight or that this problem should be consigned to the 'psychosomatic' category.

Zola concluded that attendance at the hospital had nothing to do with the seriousness of the symptom the person was suffering, but arose from the constraints of their social situations. Whether or not a person went along depended largely on the 'fit or lack of fit' of their symptom with cultural expectations. (He was looking at differences between cultural groups in the area and it seemed, for example, that those of Irish origin would regard different parts of the body as important than would those of Italian origin.)

Zola suggested that several kinds of social events would tend to encourage a person to define their symptom as part of an illness. Some unrelated interpersonal crisis in their lives had occurred to a large proportion of the patients interviewed. If their symptom interfered in some way with their social relationships, or with their work, they would be likely to seek treatment. Another person actively encouraging them could also be crucial.

So – in the premenstrual time, women's experiences of discomfort or sadness etc. have to be organized into a syndrome and socially accepted as a medical problem before the woman can be said to 'have PMT'. It is interesting that most human cultures do not seem to recognize anything equivalent to premenstrual tension: Janiger *et al.* (1972) searched anthropological records and found that they 'revealed many items pertaining to cultural myths, taboos and superstitions associated with menstruation but no report of premenstrual distress as such'.

The presence of a symptom as such does not necessarily lead us to define or treat ourselves as ill. A great number of other factors come into play in this decision. This is why it can make sense to talk about the creation and the history of premenstrual tension. We can accept that women are affected by our menstrual cycles in various ways, and that some of these effects may be unpleasant, without necessarily saying that we are therefore suffering from an illness and in need of treatment. We can choose whether or not to label the feelings we have premenstrually as signs of illness, but that choice is not necessarily made individually: cultural definitions, doctors and individual men may take that choice out of our hands. So our understandings of health and illness are not only social but *political*: that is, they relate to power. Ideas about 'female troubles', especially, affect and are affected by the ways in which women as a group are seen in a culture.

Of course, particular feelings we may have may be decidedly unpleasant: painful breasts would be the most common example of that kind. I am not suggesting that women should indulge in wishful thinking to avoid this fact. But what we do about them, how and if we treat them, depends on socially constructed definitions. Hilary Allen (1984) illustrates this point by suggesting that we might

> pose the category of 'pre-breakfast syndrome' in which to lump together all the various complaints which could ever, in any individual, be shown to appear regularly in the first hours after waking and then to subside. These could include such diverse problems as habitual hangover, morning sickness, smoker's cough, lethargy or excitability, reduced or increased libido, irritability, intellectual impairment and numerous others.

These unpleasant experiences are not in our culture understood to be a part of a disease – but we still freely acknowledge them to be real, and undesirable.

Dalton's particular definition of PMT is that absolutely any symptom, if it recurs only during the premenstrual time, constitutes the syndrome, and should probably be treated with progesterone. It seems to me that it could well be more appropriate to treat the symptoms themselves if and when they arise, rather than going for something to affect the menstrual cycle, which only controls the timing of the problems. Noticing a cyclic pattern does not prove that the cycle itself is the underlying problem.

The 'symptoms' of PMT which the doctors show most concern over – depression, anxiety and so on – are mental states which do not 'fit' with women's culturally-created notions of ourselves as nice, kind, gentle, etc. 'Mood change', as such, is often listed as a symptom – demonstrating that change *as such* is not culturally acceptable. Why *are* women's moods seen as such a problem? Men have moods too, after all. There's no evidence that women are in fact more unpredictable or inconsistent than men – it's a stereotype that men like to encourage. Couldn't it have something to do with the way that women are supposed to pander to men's moods: soothing the troubled brow, 'Did you have a good day at the office, dear?' There's just no room for women to have strong feelings of their own, disrupting this comfortable flow of emotional services.

It is interesting that in one recent survey of women attending St Thomas's Hospital's PMT clinic, when women were asked which symptoms they experienced, 'loss of libido' was the second most commonly reported 'symptom' (Taylor and James 1979). It came level with irritability and second only to depression. Cyclic change in sexual energies is defined as a symptom of sickness only in a culture which expects women to be sexually responsive to men at all times. Where health equals constant sexual availability, appealing to illness definitions may be a woman's only way out of unwanted sex.

Women do, certainly, suffer various kinds of pain as a result of their menstrual cycles: for many women period pain is a far more serious problem than PMT. But period pain is mainly a problem for the woman herself – it is not socially disruptive. If women taking time off work can be induced to lie about the reason for it, the problem can be made to disappear – unlike the symptoms' of PMT. The excitement about PMT results from 'the fact that the symptoms often spill over to affect not just the woman but also her family, her marriage and her working life' (Cooper 1977).

Ronald Taylor, who is Professor of Obstetrics and Gynaecology at St Thomas's Hospital, London, writes: 'I have known of no other condition in which so many husbands take time off to accompany their wives to the first Clinic visit' (Women's Health Care, undated). If you consider the range of painful and distressing conditions that a consultant in gynaecology would see, it does look rather as though men have some particular interest in wanting their wives' 'PMT' treated.

We do, then, have a certain amount of choice about whether or not we accept PMT as a description of our experiences of cyclic change. Feminists have raised similar questions in relation to the menopause, and to pregnancy, which doctors tend to treat as states of illness. We should think about the consequences of defining a large proportion of otherwise well women as ill because of unpleasant feelings during part of their menstrual cycle. To assert the reality of these feelings – yes, this is essential – but to decide that they are abnormal and to be stamped out . . . that is another matter.

The history of PMT

So we can see that PMT can be looked at as a construction, an idea, rather than as a 'discovery' of something already there. It is then important to see that PMT, as an idea, has a history which goes back further than its present phase of publicity.

As I have said, PMT can be compared to nineteenth-century women's illnesses, though it does not arise as a distinct category until the 1930s. It is also worth noting that much of the evidence which is used to support the case for PMT actually refers to what is called the 'paramenstruum' - which includes both the days immediately before the period, and the days of bleeding. (Dalton in particular uses this term, which is an interesting blurring of categories, since she also claims that a woman's hormonal and hence emotional state changes totally when her bleeding begins.) To the extent that this is done, PMT should be seen as a close cousin to the very widespread set of beliefs that menstruating women are dangerous to men, tend to be insane, have magical powers, and so on.

What follows, then, is an attempt to piece together a history of PMT. Basic ideas about PMT have not changed a great deal since it was first described, which was, as far as I know, by Frank in 1931. But the idea has become more sophisticated, and now that treatment with hormones is a possibility, doctors can feel that they have more to offer if they diagnose it. From the start PMT was a very vague concept: over the years doctors have claimed over 150 symptoms to be associated with a premenstrual syndrome (Moos 1968).

I took to collecting symptoms myself, to amuse myself while I ploughed through the medical literature on PMT. The resulting list goes as follows, in no special order:

weeping
tantrums
quarrels
depression
asthma
vertigo
migraine
headache
backache
epileptic fits
pain
herpes
rhinitis (runny nose)
urticaria (patches of itchy skin)
suicide
lethargy
irritability
dizziness
palpitations
bloated feelings in the abdomen and breasts
swelling in the fingers and legs
increased sexual desire
drowsiness
increased thirst or appetite
aggression

oliguria (producing too little urine)
increase in weight
spontaneous subcutaneous haemorrages (bleeding under the skin)
tightness of the clothing
stiffness of the hands
fever
ulcerative stomatitis (mouth ulcers)
transient nymphomania
pain in the breasts
emotional instability
aching in the thighs
menstrual irregularity
nausea and vomiting
pruritis vulvae (inflamed vulva)
sciatica
pains in the shoulder, knees, feet, neck
apathy
tiredness
phobic panic attacks
anger
sleeplessness
diarrhoea
constipation
feelings of intimacy
paranoid ideas
obsessive compulsive behaviour
impatience
metatarsalgia (pain in the bones of the feet)
bad breath
labial elephantiasis (extreme enlargement of the lips of the vulva)
a sense of internal shaking
feelings of well-being
apprehension
fretfulness
sluggishness
sudden outbursts of emotion
irritated eyes
reduction in hearing or temporary deafness
bleeding from the nose
crushing chest pain
rectal pressure
feeling of pressure in the bladder
hair falling out
muscle weakness
aching and cramping pain, swelling and stiffness of joints
difficulty thinking in a rational way
forgetfulness
hypersensitivity to sounds, sight and touch
stimulus-overload
sinusitis
glaucoma
tension
fainting
exhaustion
upper respiratory tract infections
tonsillitis
acne
styes
boils
hypoglycemia (low blood sugar)
hoarseness
amnesia
postural hypotension (low blood pressure on standing up suddenly)
clumsiness
alcoholism
violence
lack of concentration
illogical reactions
feelings of worthlessness.

The emphasis which has been placed on different 'symptoms' has changed somewhat, with different authors taking an interest in different 'symptoms'. For instance, as we have seen, while two

early writers said that PMT patients had nymphomania (Israel 1938; Gray 1941), women today are often treated for 'loss of libido'. The symptoms of PMT seem to be pretty flexible, perhaps depending more on what is inconvenient behaviour than on anything else.

After the first descriptions of PMT it seems to have become part of medical vocabulary, but not an important part. During the 1940s and 1950s there seems to have been most interest in PMT in relation to deviant women: female prisoners, mental patients, and so on. At this distance it is difficult to be sure of the reasons for this, since reasons are not given in the studies themselves (e.g. Morton *et al.* 1945). Certainly women in institutions constitute a convenient group on whom to experiment – this is the period of fastest expansion of the pharmaceuticals industry, and it seems likely that the idea of establishing PMT as a treatable condition would have been attractive to them.

The article now described by most writers as the beginning of the modern era for PMT was by Greene and Dalton, published in the *British Medical Journal* in 1954. From then until the present day Dalton has produced a steady stream of articles in medical journals and popularizing books and articles which attribute a wide range of problems, social and physical, to PMT (e.g. Dalton 1969). She also from the start advocated treatment with progesterone or synthetic progestogens.

Thus when in the mid to late 1970s, PMT clinics were set up, symposia held, and popular handbooks proliferated, it was principally Dalton's work which was drawn on. The majority of GPs seem to have continued throughout to pay little attention to PMT and to prescribe a variety of remedies – diuretics, exercise, fresh air, rest, etc. In a survey of six much-used 1970s gynaecology textbooks (Laws, unpublished), I found that all but one mentioned it, but only one discussed it at much length. They seemed to doubt its reality less than they doubted the reality of period pain, because, they said, weight gain gives them some 'objective' evidence of change. Their favoured remedies are tranquilizers, diuretics and progestogens, though they mention others.

Women report doctors telling them to 'get married and have a baby' (Women's Health Care) – and psychoanalysts tend to view it, like most other 'female problems' as due to a rejection of the female role. It is in contrast to these attitudes, that PMT is just another excuse used by neurotic women to make a nuisance of themselves, that Dalton and company seem pro-woman.

The most recent phase in the PMT saga has been a wave of experiments aimed at establishing its cause using recently developed hormone assay techniques, which enable one to measure the actual level of the various hormones in a woman's blood and urine. These attempts to test long-held theories have mainly found little truth in them. Dalton claims that PMT sufferers have low progesterone levels premenstrually; other doctors claim that the fault is in the levels of other hormones, or in an interaction of several. Overviews of the literature reveal that no striking and consistent difference between the hormone levels of 'PMT sufferers' and those of 'normal' women has been found (e.g. O'Brien *et al.* 1979; Munday 1977). Munday's own study found that 30 per cent of PMT patients had low levels of progesterone, but she could not demonstrate that these women suffered any worse or differently from the remaining majority.

Smith (1976) did find 'significant but very small differences in progesterone levels'. However there was no significant difference in the progesterone/oestrogen ratio and there was a large amount of overlap between the two groups. Smith stresses that 'it was noted that both the presence and the degree of depression in any cycle or in any individual are unrelated to hormone levels for that cycle or individual'.

The only study which has found a clear separation in results for PMT sufferers from those of normal women is that of M. E. Dalton (1981). A difference was found in the levels of sex hormone-binding globulin concentrations between a group of women diagnosed as having severe PMS and a control group. It is not yet clear what the significance of this finding is. The groups of women involved seem very highly selected – women in the control group are described as having *no* premenstrual symptoms, which seems a little odd when most healthy women do notice some premenstrual changes. And the 'PMT' group apparently contained some very distressed women with histories of violence, mental hospital admissions and so on. It would be interesting to see the study repeated with different groups of women.

Since the mid 1970s another, quite different, group of people have been studying menstrual cycle mood changes. Influenced by the women's liberation movement, a number of American psychologists, sociologists and other professionals have been engaged in a number of studies which basically aim to scientifically disprove the sexist 'common knowledge' about PMT (Dan *et al.* 1980; Komnenich *et al.* 1981). I cannot summarize their findings here, for they are many and complicated. Following Mary Brown Parlee's pioneering work, they have shown the inadequacies of methodology in most previous work on menstrual cycle mood changes, detailing the ways in which these studies have ensured that they find that they are looking for.

Some studies have been carried out using better methods – for example, using men as a 'control' group, giving daily questionnaires rather than relying on women's memories. It was also important that those taking part in experiments should be unaware that it was the menstrual cycle that was being studied. And using different methods did produce different results. Swandby (1981) found 'no evidence that women experience mood fluctuation across menstrual cycles', and found very large individual differences in the pattern of moods reported.

Diane Ruble (1977) did a very interesting experiment where she gave a group of women students various physical tests to persuade them that they were either in the premenstrual phase or at mid-cycle (ovulation). In fact, all the women in the experiment were somewhere between the two phases. The women were then asked to report various moods and symptoms, and those who had been persuaded that they were premenstrual reported significantly more symptoms of PMT. Cultural expectations produced a self-fulfilling prophecy.

But while some studies find that the menstrual cycle has no effect, or that its effects are created entirely by social beliefs, it will take more than this to convince women that this is all there is to it. Randi K. D. Koeske (1980) proposes a new model for understanding menstrual cycle mood changes – what she calls an 'attributional approach'. Basically she thinks it likely that what changes during the menstrual cycle is 'arousability' – that both negative and positive emotions may be increased during the premenstrual phase. Then the culture encourages us to label negative feelings 'premenstrual', while any positive feelings will be attributed to some other cause, such as a sunny day. Further research on these lines continues.

Despite these experiments, the conventional wisdom on PMT has remained in full force. No one has any interest in publishing 'negative' results. The new hormone studies are certainly not the cause of the recent excitement about PMT – their results do not seem to have had much effect on the assertions about it. I would suggest that the history of PMT must be read as a political history, and that its recent popularity might reasonably be linked to the emergence of the women's liberation movement. PMT provides an alternative kind of answer to the question: what is wrong with women's lives?

As a story of scientific 'discovery' it certainly makes little sense.

Scientific evidence?

'Scientific evidence has now firmly established that PMT has a physical cause', writes Judy Lever in *PMT, the unrecognised illness* (1980). But has it?

Scientists have addressed themselves to two issues: establishing the existence of PMT, and discovering its cause. Most energy has gone into the latter exercise, for if a cause could be found, the problem of defining PMT, and distinguishing 'true' PMT sufferers from malingering women, would be solved.

Studies which attempt to produce evidence of the existence of the syndrome have to be essentially exercises in definition since most of the 'symptoms' involved, and, of course, the consciousness of cyclic change itself, are present in all menstruating women at some time. Much of this work of definition goes on within the discipline of psychology, where people have administered large numbers of questionnaires to large numbers of women. They tend to find what they are looking for.

To demonstrate the point that the diagnosis of PMT is basically a question of definition, one needs only to look at the accounts given of the 'illness'. Wendy Cooper (1977, p. 7) even writes 'There is a striking regularity of true PMT always in the same half of the cycle (and almost always starting on exactly the same day of the cycle).' So regular cyclic change is defined as *inherently* pathological.

No account is ever given of how PMT may start or cease in the case of any individual woman, although various assertions are made about the role of pregnancy or of the absence of pregnancy. It seems not to be thought a problem worth considering *why* the hormones of vast numbers of women should fling themselves out of balance. On the other side, none of those involved in experiments on women who complain of PMT show much interest in whether the treatment they advocate has any long-term effect. The idea of women dosing themselves daily for over half the month for the rest of their menstruating lives evidently does not dismay them in the least.

It is interesting that in making the diagnosis of PMT, the most usual recommended procedure is that the woman should keep a journal of her 'symptoms'. A list of the symptoms to have is usually included – e.g. bloatedness, depression, migraine, tension, headache, backache, irritability, etc. This is a technique which mirrors that used in feminist self-help groups to try to gain a picture of women's cyclic changes, but in a distorted version. Women's self-help groups record their experiences of cyclic change as *well* women, in order that they may notice any change from their own normal pattern –

this is quite a different attitude from one where the woman starts with the expectation that there is something wrong with her and the problem is only to discover what it is. PMT journals are also kept and examined in private, making impossible the finding, which a group might make, that certain cyclic physical or mental feelings are normal for women. In the context of a woman seeking treatment for a syndrome which she already believes she has, the picture of continually changing feelings of all kinds is easily and conveniently reduced to whatever will be considered a suitable case for treatment.

Given this point about definitions, it is not surprising that the estimates given for the percentage of menstruating women who suffer PMT varies wildly from 95 to 10, depending on your source.

On the second point, seeking the cause of PMT, a considerable amount of research exists. I will not go into it in detail, since I reject the grounds on which such work is based. But such strong claims are made by those who, like Dalton, believe that lack of progesterone causes PMT that it seems worth quoting briefly from some recent 'respectable' sources, just to show that there is no one established set of facts on this issue.

In 1979, a PMT researcher, Shaughn O'Brien, wrote 'Although claims have been made for progesterone deficiency in the pathogenesis (origin and development) of the premenstrual syndrome, evidence is in fact lacking.' The one study (Bäckström and Carstensen 1974) which did find evidence of progesterone deficiency in PMT sufferers has been seriously challenged on the reliability of its methods (*Lancet* 1981; Andersch and Hahn 1982).

More recently still, Gwyneth A. Sampsom, who has carried out a controlled trial of progesterone treatment, wrote that 'It seems at present that we have no good evidence that patients suffering from premenstrual tension syndrome have abnormal progesterone levels' (1981). Reid and Yen, in their survey of the current evidence on PMT, write that:

Numerous hypotheses have been advanced to explain the PMS but a cohesive patho-physiologic formulation has yet to be established. Therapeutic dogma has been based not infrequently on anecdotal observations or the poorly controlled trials of enthusiastic investigators. (1981, p. 86)

Both the major British medical journals have published editorials emphasizing the doubt which exists about the scientific basis for claims made about PMT. In 1981, a *British Medical Journal* editorial stated that 'The results so far reported have been conflicting . . . . There is no evidence, indeed, that one treatment is more effective that the others.' *The Lancet* has published two editorials on the subject (1981 and 1983), emphasizing the problems of distinguishing PMT from normal women's experience. The latest one says 'there is still no clear understanding of what causes the "premenstrual syndrome" or even universal agreement that it exists', and argues that in future, 'much attention needs to be given to definition and methodology if we are to avoid useless expansion of the published work'.

The hormones which have been investigated include oestrogen, progesterone, prolactin and aldosterone. Individual women, both 'PMT sufferers' and 'normal' women, do have very different levels of the various hormones, of course, and these individual differences may be used to rationalize treating them, but no clear difference between the two groups has been established.

Scientific evidence has certainly *not*, therefore, firmly established that PMT exists as a medical problem, nor has it identified the 'cause' of it. Scientific evidence is not really what it's all about – women's hormone levels seem to be suspect in a way that men's are not.

It seems very likely that a few women do have some kind of disorder (or some kinds of disorders) of the menstrual cycle which really is abnormal, just as there is some group of people with problems in every organ or system in the body. The problem with nearly all the existing work on PMT is that it has no clear conception of what a normal woman, complete with normal menstrual cycle changes, is like. They work instead with sexist stereotypes. Useful 'scientific evidence' will not emerge while the scientists hold such twisted views of their 'subjects'.

Treating PMT

This section has been a nightmare to research, because the researchers and doctors involved in trying to find an 'effective' treatment for PMT seem to disagree about absolutely everything. Most of the drugs which are recommended for PMT have not been properly tested by anybody's standards, and for those trials which have taken place, there always seems to be someone who will deny their validity. An article in the *British Medical Journal* in May 1980, which denied that progesterone deficiency is responsible for PMT, set off a long correspondence in that journal in the course of which practically all the existing evidence about the treatment of PMT was challenged, one way or another. Criticism of studies included the following: that the definition of the syndrome was faulty; that the dosages of the drugs given were wrong; that trials had not been properly controlled for bias; that the wrong days of the month were being studied; that findings of past experiments were being misrepresented; that too small a sample was being used in trials; that too short a time period was being studied (O'Brien *et al.* 1980; Dalton 1980a; Sampson 1980; Martin and Downey 1980; O'Brien 1980; Dalton 1980b; Clare 1981). Although nearly all these people are firmly committed to the project of finding a treatment for PMT, the confusion that exists among them tends to confirm my point about the non-scientific basis of definitions of PMT.

Since I can see no basis for believing one person rather than another, I shall only say that there is no single treatment for PMT which is generally accepted by the medical profession to be 'effective'.

This situation is reflected in the great number and variety of treatments which are advocated for PMT. An article in the *Journal of the American Medical Association* lists some treatments which are suggested in the USA, none of which have been proved effective in a properly controlled study:

> natural progesterone; lithium carbonate; vitamin B_6; methyltestosterone (for headaches); progestogens; estrogens; oral contraceptives; minor tranquillisers: 'Relaxation for Living' classes; regular breakfasts; aspirin; orgasm; bromocriptine; scientific information and emotional support; potassium; calcium, alone or with magnesium; special diets (low-sodium, high-protein, high-fibre); amphetamines; iduprofen; and hiding in your room. (Gonzalez 1981)

Different ideas still are held in Britain, and new treatments seem to emerge with every year that passes.

By the medical profession's own standards, the best kind of clinical trial of any drug involves comparing it with a placebo. What this means is that half of the patients in the trial are given dummy pills (or whatever) which look exactly like the real ones. The idea is that this means the researcher can distinguish the effects of people thinking they are being treated from the true effects of the drug. This is necessary because a proportion of people with all kinds of complaints are found to get better if they go through a convincing pantomime of receiving treatment. With PMT, researchers report especially high rates of response to placebo treatment: at least 50 per cent in most studies (Sampson 1981). This should not surprise us – it makes sense that many women will respond well to having their complaint taken seriously. Cyclic change is real, and having the changes one goes through recognized as such is certain to be reassuring.

This makes it particularly important that PMT treatments should always be tried against a placebo, since without the comparison it is relatively easy to get the impression that a treatment is working well, simply from its placebo effect. This would lead (and I believe has led) to women being given powerful drugs unnecessarily.

The two studies, for instance, which have tried progesterone against a placebo (Smith 1975; Sampson 1979) found that it performed no better than the placebo. Smith comments that 'this finding was in contrast to our clinical impression, which indicated that some patients did benefit from progesterone injections'. Despite this sort of evidence, both Day (1979) and Dalton (1982a) have attempted to defend the reluctance of PMT doctors to carry out controlled trials of treatments by referring to the desperate state of their patients. Dalton remains so confident in the treatment she advocates that she writes that 'it is ethically wrong to include (in trials) those in danger to themselves, (and) those at risk of epileptic fits, acute asthma attacks, suicide, homicide, baby batterers, criminal damage and alcoholic bouts are automatically excluded'. But why is it ethically right to give such people drugs which have not been properly tested?

I must also make a couple of points here about the ways in which PMT treatments are promoted. It is often said of progesterone (trade name Cyclogest) that it is a 'natural' treatment, and that its effectiveness proves that PMT is caused by progesterone deficiency. First, progesterone is derived from the yam, and although it is chemically the same as the substance found in the human body, there is nothing particularly natural about dosing oneself with extra quantities of any substance found in one's body. Second, even if progesterone or the progestogens were an 'effective' PMT treatment (which is not clear), this would not prove that any deficiency existed. Although it is a common habit of thought among doctors, reasoning a diagnosis backwards from what appears to help is not a good way of distinguishing cause from effect. Unless other evidence is taken into account, a doctor's belief in a particular treatment can too easily simply perpetuate itself (Bignami 1982).

Glick and Bennett (1972) write that 'It is known that progestogens are sedative drugs', and O'Brien suggests that this action may be expected to relieve PMT symptoms (1979). Kerr *et al.* (1980), who support the use of dydrogesterone (a synthetic progestogen) also think it likely that 'a pharmacological (drug-like) action of dydrogesterone is involved in successful response rather than a form of progesterone replacement therapy'.

Another drug claimed to relate to some deficiency is pyridoxine, vitamin B_6. High-oestrogen oral contraceptives are believed to produce pyridoxine deficiency which leads to depression in some women: this use of pyridoxine led doctors to think that it might be helpful in PMT. Day and Taylor write, however, that 'There is no evidence that vitamin B_6 deficiency occurs as a result of dietary deficiency in North European countries . . . . At this stage it is our feeling that the effects of pyridoxine . . . are those of a placebo' (1981, p. 25). Reid and Yen write that in their view 'the continued use of vitamin B_6 is based mainly on theoretical grounds . . . the possibility that a cyclic vitamin deficiency exists in the PMS seems remote' (1981, p. 88). Other 'experts' disagree, but I have seen no convincing account of why such a deficiency might exist in our diet – or why some women should suffer it and others not.

There may not be much to go on in relation to these treatments, but there is even less about the myriad other preparations which are claimed to 'help'. Several new products have been launched in Britain in the last year or two aimed specifically at women, with advertising along the lines that no woman can ever be sure that she is getting enough vitamins and minerals. These, too, of course, sell themselves on how natural they are – Efamol, which is based on Evening Primose Oil, is described as 'the natural protector'. The advertising leaflet features a bizarre image of a pretty blonde woman with no clothes on (but a *lovely* hairdo) crouched in foetal pose inside an egg-like yellow oval, which is floating above the leaves of a plant.

For all I know products like these may be of use, especially to women whose diet is inadequate (though at the price they ask, women who eat badly through poverty are highly unlikely to buy them), but they are sold on threats and faith, not on hard evidence. Taking a concoction of vitamins and minerals may not be physically harmful, but what does it mean to a woman's self-respect to regard herself as constantly in need of medication?

It has recently been proposed that a feminist way of treating PMT would be for sufferers to form self-help groups (Gardner 1982). This seems a far better idea than swallowing pills in isolation, but it worries me to think of women dividing themselves up on the basis of how they experience their menstrual cycles. I believe that PMT as an idea affects and should be examined by all women, including post-menopausal and other non-menstruating women and menstruating women who do not experience major cyclic changes.

I would prefer to see PMT discussed in all kinds of women's liberation groups, women's health groups, consciousness raising groups, whatever. It could then be seen, not as an isolated issue, but in the context of a feminist analysis of how men have used menstruation and the menopause against women, of how women's sufferings in general are treated, of 'mental illness', and of how women feel about their bodies in general. Feminist discussions would not be seen as a kind of therapy, trying to 'cure' individual women, but would focus on the politics behind medical 'scientific' theories. Perhaps looking at the political aims of those involved in promoting PMT would help us to decide what our attitude to it should be, and could also help us, next time, to have some public voice on this issue.

Are the drugs safe?

Given the lack of good evidence about the effectiveness of any of the different treatments given for PMT, it seems especially important that such drugs should *do no harm*.

On this issue, the most glaring gap in the evidence is on long-term effects – no doctor has any right to tell you that any of the drugs used in PMT have been proved safe for long-term use. The progestogens are one of the two kinds of hormone in the oral contraceptive pill, and its effects as part of a combination of hormones are only now emerging, after decades of use. The long-term effects of these hormones when used alone are likely to be different, and no one knows what they will turn out to be. In terms of so-called side-effects, we have rather more information, but again the evidence is conflicting. Drug companies and some doctors tend to minimize the adverse effects women experience. Kerr *et al.* (1980) even suggest that women participating in trials of PMT treatments are particularly prone to make 'frivolous' complaints about 'side-effects'. For this reason, I will give a very full list of the toxic effects which are known to be associated with the use of some popular PMT treatments. I will concentrate on drugs promoted as specifically effective for PMT – information about the problems associated with taking the combined contraceptive Pill, tranquillizers, anti-depressants and so on is available elsewhere (e.g. Seaman and Seaman 1977; Release 1982).

This information is translated from Martindale's *Extra Pharmacopoeia* (1977). The lists given there include every adverse effect of the drugs which is known to have occurred; these do not necessarily refer to the amounts of the drugs given for PMT, for all these drugs are also used for other purposes. This is the range of known possible effects – a woman taking one of these drugs might experience any or none of these effects.

Progestogens

Progesterone injections (the pessaries would have similar effects). Trade name: Cyclogest. May produce virilization (male characteristics) in the foetus if a woman taking it gets pregnant. Acne, swelling due to the accumulation of excess fluid in the body tissues, weight gain, digestive disorders, headache and depression have occurred. There may be an eruption of itching wheals (urticaria), inflammation of the vulva, thrush, cramps, changes in libido, vaginal secretions and menstrual patterns, with unpredictable bleeding. Alterations in liver function have been reported. Injections may be painful.

Precautions: should not be used in pregnancy, undiagnosed vaginal bleeding or, unless treatment is being attempted, patients with new lumps in their breasts. Since progesterone can cause fluid retention it should be used with care in patients with heart or kidney disease. It should be given cautiously to patients with asthma or epilepsy.

Dydrogesterone Trade name: Duphaston. Toxic effects as for progesterone. It is reported not to produce virilization of the foetus.

Norethisterone Trade names: Utovlan, Primolut N, among others – also used as an oral contraceptive. Toxic effects as for progesterone. Also has androgenic (masculinizing) effects including the growth of extra hair on the body, deepening of the voice and acne. Prolonged use may produce reversible liver disturbances.

Esther Rome (1983) reports on the experiences of women prescribed progesterone at the PMS clinic in Lynnfield, Massachusetts. Supporters of the drug, she says, claim that the only side-effect is euphoria and excess energy at the beginning of the treatment.

Yet some women complain of serious yeast infections (thrush) while using vaginal suppositories, severe diarrhoea and cramping with the rectal suppositories and an excessive drop in blood pressure with the sublingual form of the drug (put under the tongue).

I have had two letters from British women who had been prescribed progestogens: one describes starting to thicken at the waist and put on weight, and getting 'thumping' headaches at night after she inserted progesterone pessaries. The other (who took dydrogesterone) developed period cramps and irregularity in her menstrual cycle – both for the first time in her life.

Bromocriptine
Trade name: Parlodel. Toxic effects: nausea, vomiting, dizziness, low blood pressure on standing up (postural hypotension). Others reported include: headache, leg cramps, nasal congestion, sedation, hallucinations, dryness of the mouth, constipation, palpitations.

Pyridoxine (vitamin B_6)
Trade name: Benadon, among others. Has no known toxic effects

(Martindale 1977). But Katy Gardner, a GP, writes to me that it is not so non-toxic, and can cause indigestion in some women, usually on high doses, 150–200 mg per day. M. G. Brush also reports that high doses can cause 'acidity' or nausea (1981).

But there have recently been reports of serious toxic effects from very high and sustained doses of pyridoxine (Shaumberg *et al.* 1983). An article in the *New England Journal of Medicine* reports the development of a loss of muscular co-ordination and severe problems of the sensory-nervous-system in seven people who had been taking daily doses of up to two *grams* or more of pyridoxine. The first sign of trouble was typically that the person became unsteady on their feet – later their hands would become numb and clumsy. They all improved after stopping taking pyridoxine.

British doctors have never recommended such high doses for PMT as these Americans had been taking (mostly without prescription). But so many people believe vitamins and anything called 'natural' to be entirely harmless that there could certainly be a temptation to take more of the tablets if a little makes no difference. A publicity leaflet for Benadon (pyridoxine tablets) is titled 'The Vitamin for Women' and is illustrated with a pretty picture of a woman in a long dress sitting reading in a cornfield. The text makes only general statements about the functions of vitamins and says nothing specifically about why it should be 'for women'. It gives no information about dosage, nor does it mention any possible adverse effects.

'Tenavoid'

I include this as an example of the 'cocktail' type of PMT remedy. 'Cocktail' products are generally good money-makers for pharmaceutical companies – the doctor will prescribe a more expensive product to avoid writing out two prescriptions. The patient need not be confronted with the fact that she is being prescribed, in this case, a tranquillizer.

'Tenavoid' is the trade name of a product which includes bendrofluazide (a diuretic, that is, an agent which increases the amount of urine produced) and meprobamate (a tranquillizer). It is advertised to doctors as avoiding the problems of hormone treatments. For this drug I will only give the list of adverse effects given in its own advertising, since the list in the *Pharmacopoeia* is extremely long.

Diuretics of this kind can produce a number of problems by interfering with the levels of glucose, potassium and uric acid in the blood and urine.

Meprobamate can produce: drowsiness, nausea, vomiting, blood disorders and high blood pressure. The advertisements also warn that this drug should not be given to epileptics or to 'people likely to become addicted to tranquillizers'.

Now it is true that many common drugs have equally alarming lists of adverse effects associated with them. But how much risk to women's health can be justified in treating PMT?

Who profits?

When I began work on this issue, several women who are familiar with the practices of the pharmaceutical industry suggested to me that I might be able to discover financial connections between the various people involved in PMT work: drug companies and doctors, for example. The inquiries I have made have not been very fruitful. For clinical trials, drugs are supplied free by their manufacturers, and Dr M. G. Brush of St Thomas's writes that 'For our clinical trials we receive short term support from the relevant pharmaceutical company. This has sometimes allowed the employment of a research assistant' (letter, 1982).

The Kerr *et al.* study (1980) thanks Duphar Laboratories Ltd (who sell dydrogesterone) for a 'research grant, for a salary for one of us (M. Munday) and for research expenses'.

A 'Panorama' programme on the involvement of drug companies in medical research (17.1.83) drew attention to the practice of drug companies paying for the publication of special supplements to medical journals on subjects they are interested in. The articles in these supplements are not refereed (checked for accuracy by independent readers) in the same way that articles in journals like the *Lancet*, the *British Medical Journal*, and the *Journal of the American Medical Association* are. The programme emphasized that one could not tell how much influence a company would be able to exert over such publications.

A number of much-quoted articles on PMT are published in two supplements to the journal *Current Medical Research and Opinion* (1977, 1979). Both supplements feature advertisements for Duphaston (dydrogesterone from Duphar) and no other advertising.

When I wrote to Katharina Dalton asking the same questions I had asked Brush and others, she reacted rather strongly. She rang up the professor of my department, my supervisor, demanding to know whether I was really a research student as I claimed and to complain that I had no right to ask her such questions. My supervisor assured her that she felt my investigations were legitimate and that I was well qualified as a student. Dalton apparently already knew the class of my degree and which university it was from! She also knew that I had written to one of the drug companies asking questions.

I later received a curt letter from Dalton. I agreed that the information she gave in this letter would be treated as confidential, so I will only say that it contained nothing to her discredit.

So I have discovered little in this area, and I think that it would be difficult to get much information. We can, however, be sure that profits are being made out of PMT treatments, for drug companies are not charitable institutions. As a multinational industry, the pharmaceuticals make higher profits as a proportion of turnover than any other industry.

It is important to remember that profits are made out of *all* kinds of medicines. When Healthcrafts introduced their 'Ladycare' range of vitamin and mineral supplements they explained that the market research had shown that 78 per cent of all such products were being bought by women. The title of the booklet they produced in response to this realization, when they began to target the marketing of vitamin supplements directly at women, was 'Women: a nutritional approach to women's problems'.

I recently recalled a story I was told quite a few years ago – whether it ever really happened I do not know. Some women from Boston Women's Health Book Collective (who wrote *Our Bodies, Ourselves*) had a meeting with a representative of Hoffman la Roche to put to him the evidence they had about the damaging effects of Valium, their top-selling product. He struck them as a highly intelligent person. He was familiar with all the research and said that Roche were moving slowly out of tranquillizers and saw vitamins as the product of the future. Roche make Benadon, a leading brand of B_6

Recent developments

Since I wrote the first versions of this article, the PMT-doctors have been busy. One major development has been the formation in 1983 of an organization which began life as a 'National Organisation of Self-help Groups dealing with PMS', now known as 'The National Association for Pre-Menstrual Syndrome'. Despite the rhetoric about self-help, this is a Dalton enterprise. The Reverend Tom Dalton ('the first husband to know relief from PMS') introduced the first meeting. He explained that developments in the States (as described in Andrea Eagan's chapter) had led him and Katharina Dalton to be anxious to establish a 'standard pattern of approach by authentic groups'. Their work is presented as protecting women from exploitation.

The style of their literature can only be described as paternalistic. They know what's good for you - and (in mild cases) it's avoiding stress, eating regularly and so forth; and (in severe cases) it's progesterone. In the course of the first meeting Dalton advised women who were having difficulty in obtaining progesterone to visit the local chemist and ask which local doctors prescribe it.

Apparently doctors often give expense as their reason for refusing to prescribe progesterone. Dalton comments that a tribunal on over-prescribing of progesterone was held in 1958 when she was a GP. The judge accepted that progesterone was a 'reasonable and necessary' treatment for PMS. She concludes that doctors are free to prescribe progesterone as much as they like.

The Association's leaflet forsees long-term use of progesterone for some women: in younger women, it says, PMS may be relieved by treatment over several months or a few years - the body will then make more for itself. But women of 35 or older 'will probably have to stay with progesterone therapy until menopause or even longer'. No side-effects or possible long-term effects of progesterone are mentioned.

The Central Management Committee has a majority of Dalton family members - out of five people, three are Katharina Dalton, her husband and her daughter. The other two committee members (referred to in the minutes by their first names, unlike *Dr* Dalton), gave a formal vote of thanks at the end of the meeting to the Dalton family, 'for their dedication to their work on our behalf and for giving of themselves and their time for the meeting'. Dalton mentioned herself that it had been suggested that she should receive the Nobel Peace Prize 'for the peace she has brought to our homes'.

Paternalism of another kind crops up in the special attention paid to male members of the association:

> The subject of the relatively small proportion of husbands present was mentioned and this was put down to work and baby-sitting for the wives present. It was noted that the husbands who were able to attend all took a very active part in the meeting and provided a very valuable contribution to the proceedings.

Their leaflet says that 'PMS can be at the root of baby battering, husband abuse, alcoholism and even suicide'.

What double-think for an organization like this to see itself as promoting 'self-help'! Surely it is the essence of self-help that people come together to define *for themselves* what their problems are and how best to deal with them? They help each other to discover what abilities and energies they have which can be used to overcome or at least to struggle against their common difficulties. Self-help groups are successful because they mobilize and direct people's desire for control over their own lives.

Dalton's organization is actually nothing to do with self-help, but aims to manipulate women into putting pressure on their doctors to accept Dalton's beliefs about PMT, and to feed them the approved pills. One can only hope that the plan may backfire – if women meet together and talk about their lives, perhaps there will be unforeseen consequences!

Dalton is not the only one who is expanding her activities. In a period of devastating cuts in government spending on the National Health Service, I have seen newspaper reports of two new PMT clinics being set up in London hospitals. I have heard from other women's health activists that PMT is beginning to be pushed in other European countries, especially Finland, Denmark, Holland and West Germany, as well as the USA. Acceptance of the notion of PMT in this country has now gone so far that one company which manufactures sanitary towels produces a promotional leaflet about it. Evidently they think that it can sell sanitary towels as well as pills and potions!

In conclusion . . . a continuum of change

All menstruating women experience cyclic change of many kinds – Southam and Gonzaga (1965) describe changes in nearly every system of the body. It is clear that some women feel these changes more intensely than others, but these changes still constitute part of a woman's being, and are not signs of sickness. Women do not have times of normality (mid-cycle) followed by times of illness (PMT and menstruation), when their hormones suddenly overcome them – the menstrual cycle forms a continuum of change, physical, mental and social. If these changes are to be examined, one must look at the positive as well as the negative changes. Looking at bias in the interpretation of study results, an editorial in the *Lancet* points out that

> With some exceptions, the data seem equally consistent with the hypothesis of a mid-cycle syndrome of lowered crime, fewer epileptic seizures, increased self-esteem and elation, and increased sexual desire and activity. It would be incomplete to say only that women perform worse at certain times in the cycle than others; their performance may at all times be better than the average performance of males on the task in question. (1981)

There is no reason why change as such should be assumed to be a bad thing.

Mary Brown Parlee, writing about the existing psychological studies of PMT (1973) points out that all of them assume some sort of base line, some normal state in relation to which women's PMT can be measured. It is never explicitly stated what this base line is or where it comes from. The male-centred image of the body cannot conceive of continuous change, and PMT forces female experience into a category it can handle – sickness. Western medicine in general works with an unrealistic idea of health – one which is more an ideal than an 'average' state. Its image of health for women is still more difficult to live up to, and our failure to fit their theories leads to large numbers of women being regarded as ill, at least some of the time.

If we are to respect ourselves as women we have to own all our states of being as parts of ourselves, even, and perhaps especially, the painful ones. If we are angry or sad before our periods, there is anger or sadness in us, and there are reasons for it. The menstrual cycle does not impose extraneous problems on a woman – it is part of her. A newspaper report about an American PMT doctor's new book tells of 'a husband's monthly heart-rending ordeal of holding his wife down on the bed until her suicidal urges have passed' (*The Daily Gleaner*, 1983). Are we really to believe that there is no problem in this woman's life except PMT?

There is no denying that many women feel worse premenstrually than they do during the rest of their cycles. Could it not be that 'PMT sufferers' should be seen as saving up the bad feelings of the whole month and feeling them intensely during the premenstrual period, rather than as having extra misery directly created by their hormones? This seems to be a more acceptable view of the menstrual cycle than one which implies that if it did not exist women would be calm, cheerful and placid at all times.

One of the recurrent images of women used in pornography shows the woman's body divided up, sectioned off into bits. The PMT theory of a woman's body is that her hormones are somehow separate from her and affect her as if from outside herself. It is frighteningly easy for us to imagine ourselves separated from our hormones. It seems easier for us to imagine being human without our femaleness than it is for a man to imagine himself without his maleness!

Many women's lives are very difficult. The word 'stress' seems totally inadequate to describe the circumstances in which women are expected to live. And women's pain is rarely taken seriously by those who are supposed to 'help'. PMT has seemed to offer a way of getting one's troubles listened to; it enables a medical solution to be found which avoids us being labelled as neurotic or inadequate. But ultimately it dehumanizes us to be forever looking inside ourselves for the cause of our problems.

The question should not be: do I have PMT? It should be: why have the changes I am used to going through with my menstrual cycle become intolerable to me? It is important to pay attention to what exactly it is that we feel when we say we feel 'premenstrual', rather than just to try to suppress the 'worst' of it. What is it that we find we can't bear at those times? If women, together, seek the answers to these questions, I would guess that we will find much that we have in common, as well as many individual differences. And what we have in common may perhaps be due more to our shared social oppression than to our biology.

In suggesting that women's feelings during their premenstrual times are valid, I do not mean that such feelings are necessarily more true than those of other times of the month, or that they should necessarily be acted upon. Maybe we could better learn to live with the knowledge that our emotional states are affected by the menstrual cycle if we could do away with the assumption that that makes us inferior to men, and makes those emotions less valid than men's.

Perhaps the most stubborn problem of PMT is the feeling of being out of control of one's emotions. Keeping track of your cycle so as to be forewarned can make this easier to cope with, certainly. But how much are we really in control the rest of the time? The interplay of mind and body is complex and is a matter of continual change – things do look different at 3 a.m. than they do in mid afternoon. We expect to have to adjust to certain changes in our bodies. That the particular kind of change we find hardest to tolerate is the one which is felt only by women is hardly surprising in a society where women are regarded as a lower form of life.

And what sort of control does a medical solution give us? Accepting the medical model of PMT implies that women cannot live their lives without medical help. We are disabled when our ability to allow for our own physical changes is denied.

PMT is a political construct. When a woman is said to have PMT, her distress or anger is invalidated. It is part of our oppression as women that if we are feeling bad we are encouraged to blame that feeling on our female bodies. The way some people use it, PMT has become a word which describes female badness, unreliability, inferiority. PMT is a medical invention and will not be useful to us in attempting to find new, positive ways of seeing our bodies.

We do need to learn about our bodies, and finding out about our menstrual cycles is one part of that. But only through a process of collective self-discovery by women can we discover what we need to know. It is very dangerous for us to feel that we must depend upon the medical profession to tell us the 'objective' truth about ourselves, because that profession is riddled with anti-woman prejudice.

Why menstruating women's lives should involve cyclic change, and often unpleasant or painful feelings which recur cyclically, is a philosophical and political problem for us all. It is not a problem which we can safely hand over to doctors to deal with.

References

T. C. Allbutt, *A System of Medicine* (Macmillan, London 1899).

Hilary Allen, 'At the mercy of her hormones: premenstrual tension and the law', *M/f*, no 9 (1984) pp. 19–44.

B. Andersch and L. Hahn, 'Bromocriptine and premenstrual tension: a clinical and hormonal study', *Pharmatherapeutica*, 3 **2**, (1982), pp. 107–13.

T. Backstrom and H. Carstensen, 'Estrogen and progesterone in plasma in relation to premenstrual tension', *Journal of Steroid Biochemistry,* 5 (1974), p. 257.

Ben Barker-Benfield, 'Sexual Surgery in late nineteenth century America', *International Journal of Health Services*, 5 (1975), p. 287.

Giorgio Bignami, 'Disease Models and Reductionist Thinking' in ed. Stephen Rose, *Against Biological Determinism* (Allison and Busby, London 1982).

British Medical Journal, editorial; 'Premenstrual Tension Syndrome', 6158 (27.1.79), p. 212.

M. G. Brush, 'The possible mechanisms causing the premenstrual tension syndrome', *Current Medical Research and Opinion*, **4** Supp. 4, (1977) pp. 9–15.

M. G. Brush, *Premenstrual Syndrome and Period Pains*, Women's Health Concern (London 1981).

A. W. Clare, letter, *British Medical Journal (BMJ)*, 20 September 1981, p. 811.

Wendy Cooper, 'A Lay View of Premenstrual syndrome', *Current Medical Research and Opinion*, **4**, Supp. 4 (1977), pp. 5–8.

The Daily Gleaner, 'Book Reports on Women's Syndrome' (quoting Ronald Norris, *Premenstrual Syndrome*), 6 October 1983, p. 7 (Fredericton, USA).

Katharina Dalton, 'Menstruation and Crime', *BMJ*, **2** (1961), p. 1752.

K. Dalton, *The Premenstrual Syndrome* (Heinemann, London 1964).

K. Dalton, *The Menstrual Cycle* (Penguin, Harmondsworth 1969).

K. Dalton, *Once a Month* (Fontana Paperbacks, London 1978).
K. Dalton, letter, *BMJ*, 5 July 1980, p. 61.
K. Dalton, letter, *BMJ*, 11 October 1980, p. 1009.
K. Dalton, 'What is this Premenstrual Syndrome?' *Journal of the Royal College of General Practitioners*, **32** (December 1982), pp. 717–23.
K. Dalton, 'Legal implications of Premenstrual Syndrome', *World Medicine*, 17 April 1982, pp. 93–4.
M. E. Dalton, 'Sex-hormone binding globulin concentrations in women with severe premenstrual syndrome', *Postgraduate Medical Journal* (September 1981) **57**, pp. 560–1.
Mary Daly, *Gyn/Ecology* (Beacon Press, Boston 1978).
Alice J. Dan, Effie A. Graham and Carol P. Beecher (eds), *The Menstrual Cycle: Vol 1. A synthesis of interdisciplinary research* (Springer Pub. Co, New York 1980).
J. B. Day, 'Clinical trials in the premenstrual syndrome', *Current Medical Research and Opinion*, **6**, Supp. 5 (1979), pp. 40–5.
J. B. Day and R. W. Taylor, 'Aetiology of Premenstrual Syndrome', in P. A. van Keep and W. H. Utian (eds), *The Premenstrual Syndrome* (MTP Press, Lancaster 1981).
Susan Edwards, *Female Sexuality and the Law* (Martin Robertson, Oxford 1981).
Barbara Ehrenreich and Dierdre English, *For Her Own Good* (Pluto Press, London 1979).
R. T. Frank, 'The Hormonal Cause of Premenstrual Syndrome', *Arch. Neurol. and Psychiatry*, **26** (1931), pp. 1053–7.
Katy Gardner, letter, *Spare Rib*, (September 1982), p. 33.
Matthew M. Garrey, A. D. T. Govan, Colin Hodge and Robin Callander, *Gynaecology Illustrated* (Churchill Livingstone, Edinburgh 1978).
Charlotte Perkins Gilman, *The Yellow Wallpaper* (Virago, London 1981).
Glick and Bennett, in R. I. Shader (ed.), *Psychiatric complications of medical drugs* (Raven, New York 1972).
Elizabeth Gonzalez, 'Premenstrual Syndrome: an ancient woe deserving modern scrutiny', *Journal of the American Medical Association*, **245**, no. 14 (1981), p. 1393.
L. A. Gray, 'Use of Progesterone in nervous tension states', *Southern Medical Journal*, **34** (1941), p. 104.

Mary Hartman and Lois Banner (eds.), *Clio's Consciousness Raised* (Harper and Row, New York 1974).
S. L. Israel, 'Premenstrual Tension', *Journal of the American Medical Association*, **110** (1938), p. 1721.
Oscar Janiger, Ralph Riffenburgh and Ronald Kersh, 'Cross-Cultural Study of Premenstrual Symptoms', *Psychosomatics*, **13** (1972), pp. 226–35.
Sir Norman Jeffcoate, *Principles of Gynaecology* (Butterworths, London 1975).
G. D. Kerr, J. B. Day, M. R. Munday, M. G. Brush, M. Watson and R. W. Taylor, 'Dydrogesterone in the treatment of the premenstrual syndrome', *The Practitioner*, **225** (1980), p. 852–5.
Beryl Kingston, *Lifting the Curse* (Ebury Press 1980).
Randi K. D. Koeske, 'Theoretical Perspectives on Menstrual Cycle Research', in Alice Dan *et al.* (eds.), *The Menstrual Cycle: Vol 1* (1980).
P. Komnenich, M. McSweeney, J. A. Noack and N. Elder (eds.), *The Menstrual Cycle: Vol 2, Research and implications for women's health* (Springer Pub. Co, New York 1981).
Lancet, editorial: 'Premenstrual Syndrome', **2** (8260–1) (19–26 December 1981), pp. 1393–4.
Lancet, editorial: 'Premenstrual uncertainties', **2** (8356) (22 October 1983), pp. 950–1.
JudyLever, *PMT: the unrecognised illness* (New English Library, London 1980).
Martin and Downey, letter, *BMJ* (23 August 1980), p. 562.
Martindale, *The Extra Pharmacopoeia* (The Pharmaceutical Press, London 1977; reprinted 1979).
R. H. Moos,'The development of the Menstrual Distress Questionnaire', *Psychosomatic Medicine*, **3**, 30 (1968), p. 853.
J. H. Morton, H. Addison, R. G. Addison, L. Hunt and J. J. Sullivan, 'A Clinical Study of Premenstrual Syndrome', *American Journal of Obstetrics and Gynecology*, **65**, 6 (1945), p. 1183.
Madeleine Munday, 'Hormone levels in severe premenstrual syndrome', *Current Medical Research and Opinion,* **4**, Supp. 4 (1977), pp. 16–22.
Shaughn O'Brien, letter, *BMJ* (17 March 1979).
P. M. S. O'Brien, letter, *BMJ* (23 August 1980).
P. M. S. O'Brien, D. Craven, C. Selby and E. M. Symonds, 'Treatment of premenstrual syndrome by Spirolactone', *British*

Journal of Obstetrics and Gynaecology, **86** (1979), p. 142.

P. M. S. O'Brien, C. Selby and E. M. Symonds, 'Progesterone, fluid and electrolytes in premenstrual syndrome', *BMJ* (10 May 1980), p. 1161.

Mary Brown Parlee, 'The Premenstrual Syndrome', *Psychological Bulletin*, **80**, 6 (1973), pp. 454–65.

M. B. Parlee, 'Stereotypic Beliefs about Menstruation: a methodological note on the Moos MDQ and some new data', *Psychosomatic Medicine*, **36**, no. 3 (May–June 1974), pp. 229–40.

I. H. Pearse and L. H. Crocker, *The Peckham Experiment* (Allen and Unwin, London 1949).

Isaac Ray, *Mental Hygeine*, (facsimile of 1863 edition) (Häfner Publishing Co., New York 1968).

Robert L. Reid and S. S. C. Yen, 'Premenstrual Syndrome', *American Journal of Obstetrics and Gynaecology*, **139**, no. 1 (1981), p. 85.

Release, *Trouble with Tranquillisers* (Release Publications, London 1982).

Silvia Rodgers, 'Women's Space in a Men's House: the British House of Commons', in Shirley Ardener (ed.), *Women and Space* (Croom Helm, London 1981), pp. 50–71.

Esther Rome, 'PMS examined through a feminist lens', unpublished paper, given at Society for Menstrual Cycle Research Conference, San Francisco, May 1983.

Diane N. Ruble, 'Premenstrual Symptoms: a reinterpretation', *Science*, **197** (1977), pp. 291–2.

Diane Ruble, quoted in Mary Brown Parlee, 'New Findings: menstrual cycles and behaviour', *Ms*, **XI** no. 3 (September 1982), pp. 126–8.

Gwyneth A. Sampson, 'Premenstrual syndrome: a double blind controlled trial of progesterone and placebo', *British Journal of Psychiatry*, **135** (1979), pp. 209–15.

G. A. Sampson, letter, *BMJ* (5 July 1980).

G. A. Sampson, 'An appraisal of the role of progesterone in the therapy of the premenstrual syndrome', in P. A. van Keep and W. H. Utian (eds.), *The Premenstrual Syndrome* (MTP Press, Lancaster 1981).

Barbara Seaman and Gideon Seaman, *Women and the crisis in sex hormones* (Bantam Books, New York 1977).

G. S. Siegel, *Periodic Health Examinations – Abstracts from the literature*, Public Health Service Publication no. 1010 (US Govt Printing Office, Washington DC 1963).

Richard I. Shader and Jane I. Ohly, 'Premenstrual tension, femininity and sexual drive', *Medical Aspects of Human Sexuality* (April 1970), p. 48.

Herbert Shaumberg, Jerry Kaplan, Anthony Windebank, Nicholas Vick, Stephen Rasmus, David Pleasure and Mark J. Brown, 'Sensory Neuropathy from Pyridoxine Abuse: a new megavitamin syndrome', *New England Journal of Medicine*, **309**, no. 8 (25 August 1983), pp. 445–8.

S. L. Smith, 'Mood and the menstrual cycle', in E. J. Sachar (ed.), *Topics in Psychoendocrinology* (Grune and Strathan, New York 1975).

S. L. Smith, 'The Menstrual Cycle and Mood Disturbances', *Clinical Obstetrics and Gynaecology*, **19**, no. 2 (1976) pp. 391–7.

Social Trends 1984 (Central Statistical Office, Her Majesty's Stationery Office, London 1984).

A. L. Southam and F. P. Gonzaga, 'Systemic changes during the menstrual cycle', *American Journal of Obstetrics and Gynecology*, **91** (1965), pp. 142–65.

Miriam Stoppard, *Everywoman's Lifeguide* (Macdonald 1982).

Janet R. Swandby, 'A Longitudinal Study of Daily Mood Self-reports and their relationship to the Menstrual Cycle', in Komnenich *et al.* (eds.), *The Menstrual Cycle: Vol 2* (1981).

R. W. Taylor and C. E. James, 'The clinician's view of patients with the premenstrual syndrome', *Current Medical Research and Opinion*, **6**, Supp. 5 (1979), pp. 46–51.

Paula Weideger, *Female Cycles* (Women's Press, London 1978).

Women's Health Concern, *Premenstrual Syndrome* (pamphlet), self-published (London undated).

Erna Wright, *Periods Without Pain* (Tandem Books, London 1975).

Irving Kenneth Zola, 'Culture and Symptoms: an analysis of patients' presenting symptoms', *American Sociological Review*, **31** (1966), p. 615.

I. K. Zola, 'Pathways to the Doctor: from person to patient', *Social Science and Medicine*, 7 (1973).

3 Getting away with murder: PMT and the press

Valerie Hey

Preface

In November 1981, Christine English was tried and discharged on the count of manslaughter. Throughout the trial, her successful defence was based on the claim that she was not responsible for her actions. Her defence counsel was able to use this argument because she suffered from a severe condition of PMT. This article will briefly survey some of the key themes used by newspaper journalists in their reporting of this trial and verdict. It will also provide opportunities to see how the other factors at play in the trial construct one condition of PMT, and one category of PMT sufferers. I will also try to reveal an underlying impulse to depict all females as biologically unreliable, since a generalizing tendency within these discourses is to cast serious doubts on all women's 'sanity'.

I will not engage with the medical arguments concerning the 'existence' of the pre-menstrual syndrome. The article will simply attempt to show the ideological effectiveness of PMT, working both to secure Christine English's release and to secure all women's capture within the harmful and debilitating categories of 'hormones and hysteria'.

Introduction

Some years ago, I read *Once a Month* (Dalton 1978), one of Katharina Dalton's popular PMT 'rationales', and a friend lent me another PMT manifesto. At the time, I found both books disquieting; however, it was not until I read the press coverage of Christine English's trial and subsequent conditional discharge from the charge of manslaughter on the grounds of 'diminished responsibility due to pre-menstrual tension', that my disquiet took on a more political character. Dalton's book is an analysis of the causes and effects of PMT with advice on self-help and medical remedies.

Initially, both books had made me suspicious, mainly because of their enthusiastic insistance on reducing the complex experience of our menstrual lives to the modern equivalent of the bubonic plague. Nowhere in this ideology of PMT could I find anything positive or even ambivalent about menstruation. We were told that for some women, PMT descended with devastating consequences, causing a radical rupture in an otherwise contented and passive existence. I couldn't fit this to my own premenstrual experience – it is a state which I find full of mixed feelings and one that includes an increased sensitivity to stimuli, increased libido and sensuality. I don't think I am unique in this, for I think that most women are aware of a sense of continuous change as part of how we experience the world of our bodies. The ideology of PMT only allows us to experience ourselves as either nothing – 'one of the lucky ones' – or as a biological time-bomb waiting to go off.

When I read and re-read the newspaper accounts of the English case, and when I read them today, what shocks me is the misogyny that they reveal. They suggest a fear and loathing directed at all women, provoked by our difference and 'otherness'. I am now certain, convinced by Sophie Laws's arguments in the second chapter (written independently of my own work) that PMT is a harmful and controlling paradigm; a mechanism for dealing with our 'difference'. Its crude biologism allows for women's different and therefore 'dangerous' bodies to be disqualified.

A good example of the way PMT is used by patriarchal medical discourse is provided by Dr Rowland Berry, a therapist at an all-women borstal. During an interview, Polly Toynbee remarked, that the existence of an all-male hierarchy in the borstal might be detrimental to the women's sense of self-esteem: 'Good God, you couldn't have all women!' came the reply. 'The place would be rife with pre-menstrual tension and no sanity anywhere!' (*Guardian*, 14.3.83).

Any further postponement of asking questions about the outcome of this trial concedes even more ground to a virulent antifeminism which cannot wait to dance around our long-suspected bodies.

Women's reluctance to ask questions about the effectiveness of our specific biology and physiology is not surprising, however, in a culture which throughout time has deemed our bodies faulty and polluting. Foucault identifies this historical processing of female sexuality into what he terms as 'a hysterization of women's bodies' – a strategic unity which involves 'a threefold process, whereby the feminine body was analysed, qualified and disqualified' (Foucault 1981). To be female is a handicap; a burden to be endured with its vulnerability to maternity and to the 'curse' of menstruation.

Consequently, to argue that our specifically female bodies have specific consequences, possibly requiring specific differential responses, seems to be an impossibility in an historical moment which is all too keen to consign us to the kitchen or the nursery.

The central question of how far we can afford to acknowledge our differing bodies is not merely a medical matter. It is a political question, and one that has resulted in an impasse within the various forms of feminism. One body of opinion sanctions our 'otherness' from men and argues that male oppression has severed us from our innate femaleness; another refuses to think that our bodies have any effectiveness of that the difference between male and female bodies amount to the degree of difference to be found between soap powders.

Ultimately, this question of the significance of the different physical bodies of men and women will have to be addressed in terms that rescue women from earth mother mysticism *and* from bodiless politics. I suggest that this project becomes even more vital as biological determinism (i.e. *non*-feminist variety) promotes itself as the new wisdom, replete with its gurus (Desmond Morris, Lionel Tiger, etc.) and keen to provide the fictional sell for the monetarist endeavour.

I know 'times is hard', the climate of 'money terrorism' and 'Victorian virtues' saps confidence, but we have to move into the argument before the whole question is answered in terms that harm us as women.

Some key questions that arise from a consideration of this case include the following:

1 If we view the PMT package as a dangerous simplification of how we experience our menstrual cycles, how can we begin to think about such capacities and deal with their negative and positive aspects?
2 If we don't develop a more sophisticated approach and if we deny the importance of menstruation, we are guilty of leaving women who suffer from its effects isolated, individualized and silenced – a relatively powerless group, who can be delivered up to the controlling strategies of hormone intervention.[1]* Dalton's dosages of progesterone appear as 'solutions' precisely because no one else has even bothered to take menstrual complications seriously.
3 How are we successfully to support women with menstrual difficulties in a culture that can co-opt such an argument to deny women's right to be treated as an equal?

These are only some of the problems posed by the English case. The list is obviously not exhaustive.

A short survey of press reactions to English's acquittal will provide a useful insight into male–female relations; female biology and behaviour and its interpretation and social construction in judicial, medical and journalistic discourse. Press reaction falls into two main areas which I would now like to discuss.

First, I look at how the implications of English's acquittal are managed by the individual legal spokesperson and then how the press represents the alarm over women's violence in a manner which simultaneously seeks to sensationalize while producing a particular meaning of women as possessors of pathologically suspect bodies.

Second, I examine how the tying of women's unpredictable behaviour to our biology presents ideological rewards to a patriarchal society that prefers us medicalized rather than radicalized. Thus to describe our premenstrual time only as illness and one that if unsupervised by experts can explode in violence obstructs a theorization of our 'tension' as external to ourselves and feeds into our socially produced tendency for self blame.

---

* Superior figures refer to the Notes section at the end of this chapter.

Theme one . . . 'An Excuse for Anything': Nina Kitson[2]

The successful defence of Christine English was based on her claim to be 'suffering from an aggravated form of what is known as pre-menstrual syndrome' (*Guardian*, 11.11.81). The chief defence expert witness testified that 'Mrs English had suffered from it since 1966. It made her tired, cry easily, lose her temper and make her liable to throw things – it could happen in a split second' (Dalton, *Guardian*, 11.11.81). It was ascertained that, on the day in question, Christine English had not eaten anything and the same witness claimed that 'the syndrome had caused an accumulation of adrenalin in the blood and changes in the body hormones which led to irritability, aggressiveness, impatience and loss of self-control' (Dalton, *Guardian*, 11.11.81).

Several articles draw connections between the English case and the outcome of the Smith case earlier in the same week. The links between these two cases were introduced in the following terms: '. . . a second woman was freed by a court yesterday . . . ' (*Guardian*, 11.11.81) or 'it was the second case in two days in which a "monthly miseries" defence led to a woman being released after committing an act of violence' (*Sun*, 11.11.81).

On Monday 9 November, Sandie Smith was tried at the Old Bailey for threatening to kill a policeman while carrying a knife. She was already on probation for stabbing to death another barmaid, and had a large number of previous convictions, all said to be related to her times of premenstrual tension. She was already being treated with daily injections of progesterone, without which her defence counsel said she 'became a raging animal each month'. She was given a further term of probation and was ordered to continue with medical treatment.[3]

This 'syndrome' is obviously no respecter of social class, for we are informed that Christine English 'has a degree in English literature' while Sandie Smith was a 'barmaid' (*Guardian*, 11.11.81). Given its frequent occurrence, 'PMT affects an estimated four million women' (*Guardian*, 11.11.81) and 'it is the commonest disease of all, affecting four out of ten women to some extent'. (Dalton, *Sunday Times*, 15.11.81) The defensive and panic-ridden tones that structure the reporting of the case become more understandable. The chief concern of these accounts centres on the main implication of the case – the 'excuse' that severe PMT is seen to offer women as a legitimate exemption from the legal consequences of violent behaviour.

The *Guardian* report of 11 November opens with a blandly factual statement of the outcome of the case, immediately followed by a warning (one of many that pepper the article). This opening admonishment is delivered on behalf of the 'medical profession' by Gerald Swyer, Chairman of Women's Health Concern, who is quoted as saying 'it was unbelievable that women in the premenstrual phase of the cycle can kill someone and get away with it'.

As if almost to anticipate and forestall these sweeping anxiety-ridden accusations, the defence counsel, Mr Rant, tactfully and tactically paints Christine English as a 'special case'. He is reported as insisting that 'I am not saying that this opens the door for every woman who suffers from mild PMT. It does not' (*Daily Mirror*, 11.11.81). This was a point addressed and endorsed by the judge: 'I am satisfied that you committed this offence in wholly exceptional circumstances' (*Guardian*, 11.11.81). Significantly, it is the *only* one of the judge's statements to be reported and, within the text, it serves to stress the uniqueness of the English acquittal. However, it is the tension between the claims for its 'exceptionality' and the potentiality for its expression in the bodies of menstruating women that plagues the male writers.

The tension plays across all the discourses. Thus, while it is acknowledged that the use of PMT as a defence 'has not always succeeded' (*Guardian*, 11.11.81), and that both Christine English and Sandie Smith suffered from acute forms of the syndrome, the collusive impact of the articles is to seek a 'disciplining' of all women, and a consequent subversion of the Crown's response to the English case.

It is almost as if men, fearing the anger of women, arrange a set of defensive strategies before women begin to claim a right to clemency under the protection of having severe PMT. This is not precisely what I want to express, since it implies a crude conspiracy model operating, but I don't know how else to convey the strategies, whether conscious or not, that so consistently produce such observable effects: the language used is filled with threats, warnings, anxieties and just plain old-fashioned fear, while its tone is hectoring and disciplinarian.

For example, if we look at the way the case was presented in the *Sun*, (11.11.81), we can see how this fear of female violence is invoked and revoked. Visually, the page is split into two main sections. Two-thirds are devoted to 'Monthly miseries save the killer mistress' and one-third entitled 'Ten ways to help yourself – a guide to beat the blues'. The principle headline is written in the style of the 'crime passionel', only this time the roles are reversed and we are told unequivocally in the case of Christine English that 'pre-menstrual tension *made* her kill her lover' (*Sun* 11.11.81; my emphasis).

The impulse to 'mow down her lover' (*Sun*, 11.11.81), is reduced to a biological urge. It is this fact that is given priority in the reporting while other data are relegated to being mere background 'colour' and are not utilized as explanations for Christine English's 'loss of self control'. I will return to this point later in an analysis of why PMT is a 'useful' paradigm for 'explaining' female violence or 'deviance'.

Adjacent to this portrayal of a biological bombshell – or a 'blonde divorcee' as the *Sun* prefers – we read a 'do-it-yourself' manual for controlling the 'Monthly Miseries' before they escalate to the status

MONTHLY MISERIES SAVE THE KILLER MISTRESS

Freed . . . mother-of-two Christine English, who killed her lover

By IAN HEPBURN

ATTRACTIVE Christine English walked to freedom yesterday after a court accepted that pre-menstrual tension made her kill her lover.

It was the second case in two days in which a "monthly - miseries" defence led to a woman being released after committing an act of violence.

She mowed down lover

Mother-of-two English, 36, drove her car at her live-in lover after he threatened to end their affair.

She slammed her foot on the accelerator—and the car carried 30-year-old Barry Kitson across the entrance to a supermarket.

Then English ran over him, almost severing one of his legs. Mr Kitson died two weeks later.

Yesterday a doctor told Norwich Crown Court that premenstrual tension had made English lose her self-control.

Clasping

She has suffered from the condition since 1966, said Harley Street specialist Katarina Dalton.

"It would make her irritable, aggressive, impatient, and confused, with loss of self-control," added Dr Dalton.

English, of Greenstead Estate, Colchester, Essex, denied murder, but admitted manslaughter on the grounds of diminished responsibility.

She was given a conditional discharge for 12 months and banned from driving for a year.

The blonde divorcee left the court clasping the hand of probation officer Brian Harrison.

She said: "I am very relieved it is all over. Now I just want to get back to my family."

Prosecutor John Alliott, QC, said English had lived with Mr Kitson for three years.

Last December his interest in her cooled and he announced his intention to meet another woman.

Mr Alliott said: "She became angry and upset. She phoned Mr Kitson's mother threatening to kill him and run him over."

On the day English carried out the threat, Mr Kitson had been drinking in a pub called the Live And Let Live.

Victim Barry . . . wante to end the affair

When he came o they rowed. He slap ped her and pulled h hair.

Mr Kitson went another pub and, ou side, met his death.

Knife

Later English to police: "He turned a made a V-sign at me. just wanted to bur him and hurt him."

● **AT** the Old Bailey Monday, a woma whose pre-menstru tension turned her in a "raging animal" w freed for the secor time.

Sandie Smith, from Leyton, East Lo don, was put on pr bation for threateni police with a knife.

Ten ways to help yourself

By MARGARET FARRALL

A guide to beat the blues

HERE are ten ways women suffering from PMT can ease their problem. Hormone treatment can be given by your doctor. But these rules may be all you need.

● **Take vitamin B6 tablets, bought from the chemist. Just before a period the body runs short of this vitamin — when it is most needed.**

● **Drink mild herbal teas fruit juices or mineral water instead of strong tea and coffee.**

● **Eat little and often, foods, like meat—particularly liver—eggs, cereals, wholemeal bread, rice and yeast.**

● **Don't eat sugary things like chocolate and biscuits and cut down on salt because it makes your body retain water, making you feel bloated and tired.**

● **Don't take on heavy stressful jobs on your bad days.**

● **Exercise and get lots of fresh air.**

● **Talk about it to your husband and family.**

● **Buy or borrow a book on PMT. Knowing is understanding and you will probably recognise symptoms and learn how to treat them.**

Pressure

● **Arrange for a friend to look after the children for an hour or so to ease your pressure.**

● **Take time to put your feet up and relax.**

of a 'hormonal disease which affected the mind' (*Daily Mirror*, 11.11.81). The implication is very clear – that Christine English demonstrates a failure in self-regulation. If only she had heeded the section in the guide entitled 'Pressure', which advises: 'arrange for a friend to look after the children for an hour or so .... Take time to put your feet up and relax' – individual 'solutions' to this 'individual physiological condition' that remain completely abstracted from the material reality of most women's lives.

Theme Two . . . 'not responsible for herself':
Mr James Rant QC[4]

In separating Christine English from the consequences of her actions an effective defence was built around her susceptibility to PMT. It was established by her defence counsel that the prime deteminant of her actions was her uncontrolled body, the hormonal imbalances of which defeated the rational control of her mind. 'Something in her snapped' and 'in wholly exceptional circumstances' (*Guardian*, 11.11.81) Mrs English 'killed her lover by deliberately running him down with her car' (*Daily Mirror*, 11.11.81).

Apart from the obvious practical gains that her defence counsel was able to obtain from arguing her susceptibility to PMT, there is a more complex ideological and social aspect to the argument, which illuminates a set of spoken/unspoken assumptions concerning masculinity and femininity.

At the level of 'common sense' one inevitable focus of the newspaper reports was on the 'tension that made a woman kill'. (*Daily Mirror*, 11.11.81) ' "Tense" woman freed after killing' (*Guardian*, 11.11.81); 'killer with menstrual tension freed' (*Daily Telegraph*, 11.11.81). This was the chief mitigating argument used by the defence. It won the release of the defendant and predictably influenced all the newspaper accounts. However, what I wish to record is the hermetic quality of the 'debate' on 'non-feminine' behaviour.

For PMT's use is not only in keeping individual women out of prison, but its wider political and ideological use, as an 'excuse'/ explanation for female violence is obvious.

There is something quite reassuring, I propose, to a male lawyer,

DAILY Mirror

Wednesday, November 11, 1981 14p ★

Judge frees lover after hearing of period problem

FREE: Christine English Picture: PETER CASE

THE TENSION THAT MADE A WOMAN KILL

By PETER KANE

BETRAYED mistress Christine English killed her lover by deliberately running him down with her car.

But yesterday she walked free from court after a judge heard that she had been suffering from premenstrual tension, heightened by lack of food.

A doctor had told the court that, because Mrs English's period was due, she was more violent and unstable than other women.

The judge set her free by granting her a conditional discharge. Mrs English, of Rochdale Way, Colchester, Essex, was banned from driving for a year.

Mrs English's lover, Barry Kitson, 31, died after she picked him up in her car from a pub called the "Live and Let Live", in Colchester.

Kitson, an alcoholic, punched her when they quarrelled in the car about his drinking and his other women.

He jumped out and stormed off into the darkness saying: "I hate you and never want to see you again ..."

Mrs English snapped—and moments later her car hurtled at high speed towards him as he crossed a road.

Mrs English ran into the road, screaming hysterically: "Please tell me it's not true—please God tell me it didn't happen."

Kitson was crushed against a telegraph pole and later died in hospital.

Afterwards, Mrs English, a 37-year-old divorcee, said: "I just snapped. I only wanted to frighten him."

Harley Street specialist Katherina Dalton told Norwich Crown Court that Mrs English suffered from premenstrual tension syndrome—a hormonal disease which affected the mind.

Before the killing, Mrs English had not eaten for nine hours, and this would have made the condition worse.

"We are talking about something more serious than what women normally suffer," said Dr Dalton.

Defending counsel James Rant, QC, said: "I am not saying that this case opens the door for every woman who suffers from mild premenstrual tension. It does not.

"But it would not serve

● Turn to Page Three

The tension that killed

● From Page One

society if Mrs English were to go to prison."

Mr. Justice Purchas told Mrs. English that he recognised she had suffered great remorse and he was sure she was not a danger to the public.

That was why, he said, he was able to free her.

Mrs. English's plea of not guilty to murder had been accepted by the prosecution. She had admitted manslaughter on the grounds of diminished responsibility.

Last night, Mrs. English, a mother of two said: "I am just relieved it is all over.

"I don't think it would have served any purpose to lock me up.

I have punished myself over and over again. I lie awake at night and I can't get the thought of it out of my mind.

"I never wanted to kill him. I still carry his picture with me."

Last night, Mr. Kitson's widow, Nina, said: "Other women have to learn to live with and control premenstrual stress and tension.

"It seems wrong that women can now use this as an excuse for anything."

Mirror Science Editor Ronald Bedford writes: This case underlines the new view that British courts are taking towards the problem of premenstrual tension.

There is mounting medical evidence to show that, at certain times of the month, and for no other reason, some women can go berserk.

KITSON: He died after boasting of other women.

judge, doctor and journalist to be in possession of an account of female behaviour that directly connects it to hormonal 'irregularity'.

I am not suggesting that relief is all they feel; I have already cited instances of acute anxiety regarding their apprehension about women's volatile bodies. PMT is also a many-headed beast which can be warned against ('there is mounting medical evidence to show that at certain times of the month, and for no other reasons, some women can go berserk', *Daily Mirror*, 11.11.81). Simultaneously, vast opportunities are presented to the medical profession and endorsed by the legal profession, to control women's behaviour both medically and socially.

The PMT paradigm is a way of viewing female 'tension' that relegates all other considerations to the bottom of the check list: '*and for no other reason*, some women can go berserk' (my emphasis). Typically hysterical, the loose language of the *Daily Mirror* (11.11.81) encapsulates the ideology of women's anger/madness as *solely* reducible to her menstrual capacity. Other socio-physiological, psychological, environmental, historical or political 'causes' do not even have to be considered. If we look at a particular instance of the 'permission' that PMT offers to the 'experts', I think that the point I am trying to make will become clearer. In the *Sunday Times* (15.11.81), the medical reporter Oliver Gillie records this example of the attempt at the total medicalization of one woman: Sandie Smith, the 'raging animal' of other descriptions. This is how her 'treatment' is described.

> She (Katharina Dalton) is able to control Sandie's bizarre behaviour by hormone injections. But there are still problems. One day Sandie's period fell on a Sunday and a new district nurse forgot to give the treatment on schedule. Sandie threw a brick through a window and phoned the police. On another occasion, she did not eat for two days; this brought on symptoms despite the injections and she committed another offence.

Are we seriously to believe that Sandie Smith's actions are only related to and explicable in terms of her hormones? While Katharina Dalton complacently promotes the monocausal view that 'hormones are the answer' (see caption/quote, *Sunday Times*, 15.11.81), haven't we got to investigate the power relations within which such 'problems' and 'solutions' are proposed?

Sandie's 'problems' add up to a long list of violent and anti-social behaviour.

> She had 30 previous convictions including one of manslaughter for stabbing a friend to death. Other convictions were for criminal damage, theft, trespassing, and writing threatening letters. While in prison, she had attempted suicide by hanging, strangling and cutting her wrists. (*Sunday Times*, 15.11.81)

While it could not be claimed that this catalogue of desperate acts represents a 'normal' career – what makes it 'bizarre' seems to be her gender. Are women's 'non-feminine' actions more likely to be interpreted by a medical model because we cannot accept that women commit such acts for very much the same reasons as men? Or is it that women have reasons apart from biology to account for violent criminal and destructive responses?

I should like now to take the analysis one step further and try to show how explanations of PMT mesh in with current ideologies regarding normal male and female behaviour. The use of the concept in the defence and reporting of Christine English's case shows how the respective discourses both create and contribute to a particular, paradoxical view of women as both passive *and* hysterical. The proposition of biologically induced 'violence' offers an opportunity to explain the transition from one state to the other 'and it could happen in a split second' (Guardian, 11.11.81).

If the categories of femininity and violence are deemed to be as mutually exclusive as socialism and the Parliamentary Labour Party, then we have to explain *women's* violence, because it totally contradicts the accepted view of femaleness. What could be more ironic or convenient to secure an explanation and a solution within the very fact of women's difference, viz:

> Women do suddenly change their minds in a way men don't . . . . Their moods can change suddenly, and hormones may be responsible. The word 'hysteria' literally means a condition caused by the womb and 'lunacy' refers to the monthly cycle. (Dalton, quoted in the *Sunday Times*, 15.11.81.)

In a misogynist culture such as ours, where male violence is endemic and of epidemic proportions, it is hard to take the 'problem' of female violence seriously, or as seriously as the discourses themselves suggest we should. Yet that is precisely what we, as readers, are enjoined to do:

1 Ten ways to help yourself (the *Sun*)
2 . . . committing an act of violence (the *Sun*)
3 She was more violent and unstable than other women (*Daily Mirror*)
4 She was not a danger to the public (*Daily Mirror*)
5 The taking of life is a matter of utmost gravity. I am not submitting this as an open door for women (*Daily Telegraph*).

While I concede that the 'natural' tendency of articles reporting the killing of a male by a female is to structure the narrative to address the question of 'female violence', this naturalness hides a great deal of ideological work. The event is reported in a way which suggest that the woman's body is pathologically out of control, while at the same time suggesting that this same erring body is the sole cause of the event. As a result, female violence is neatly reduced to female biology, and questions concerning male behaviour, male violence and male practices are not even asked. Specifically, why did Kitson's provocative violence surface in the texts as merely incidental?

There are other readings of the reports which can produce more substantial explanations for the absence of a more complex analysis. If we return to the picture of Christine English as an aggravated PMT victim we find a fascinating image: 'The syndrome had caused an accumulation of adrenalin in the blood, and changes in the body hormones which led to irritability, aggressiveness, impatience and loss of self control' (*Guardian*, 11.11.81), a description which unwittingly reproduces contemporary notions and experiences of masculinity.

In other words, how we think of masculinity, men, male practices is in terms of the exercise of power supported by institutional, ideological and, on occasion, physically violent coercion. The categories of men/power/violence are frequently simply interchangeable; so much so that at times it is this very seamlessness that resists any critique. Because male violence is *not* acknowledged as separable from masculinity it is assumed to be intrinsic. It is what men are and doesn't need explaining.

In conclusion I should like to return again to the narrative details of this particular case, since it amplifies the theoretical/moral questions I am attempting to depict.

I've already noted how a utilization of a PMT defence marginalizes other possible sources of female anger, and this is aptly demonstrated in the Christine English case. By all accounts Kitson, her former lover, was a far from attractive individual, and on the day he was killed they were both involved in a long and bitter argument in which 'Kitson, an alcoholic, punched her when they quarrelled in the car about his drinking and his other women' (*Daily Mirror*, 11.11.81), and, according to the *Sun* (11.11.81), 'On the day English carried out the threat, Mr Kitson had been drinking in a pub called The Live and Let Live. When he came out, they rowed, he slapped her and pulled her hair.' In a statement made to the police, Christine English is reported as saying 'He turned and made a V-sign at me. I just wanted to bump him and hurt him' (*Daily Mirror*, 11.11.81).

No perspective is placed on these events. Within the reports, they are offered as bits of personal biography. It was *she* who 'snapped'. His provocative gestures, language and demeanour, as well as his physical assaults, retain the status of background 'colour'. The result is an acquittal for Christine English on the grounds of diminished responsibility, a consequent problematizing of women's bodies, and a *non*-problematizing of male behaviour.

If we leave the last word to Katharina Dalton, I think that she expresses more eloquently than I can the inherent limitations and political dangers that surround any simple view that women's bodies equal hysteria. She is ostensibly making a medical point about the most effective form of progestogens:

> Only the suppositories will do. The synthetic progestogens in the Pill relieve menstrual pain, but they do not reach the *violence centre(s) of the brain* and relieve the symptoms of pre-menstrual tension. (Quoted in the *Sunday Times*, 15.11.81, my emphasis.)

Postscript

Sandie Smith later appealed against her conviction, but her appeal was rejected by the Central Criminal Court on 27 April 1982. Lord Justice Griffiths said that 'PMT (was) wholly unacceptable as a defence to any crime. The sentence of a probation order accompanied by medical supervision had been merciful and proper' (*Guardian*, 28.4.82). The judges suggested that legal charges should be pursued in Parliament. Ms Smith was refused permission to appeal to the Lords, but said after the hearing that she would continue to press for a change in the law (*The Times*, 28.4.82.)

Notes

1 See correspondence in *Spare Rib* (122) September 1982 from J. Dickey, whose reservations concerning Dalton's 'wonder' cure progesterone seem well founded. She also describes a talk delivered by the doctor . . .

> The theme of the talk was that some women chronically (as opposed to occasionally) display 'anti-social' and 'bizarre' behavioural characteristics in the two weeks before their period: they get angry, upset, disruptive, even violent with their husbands! This concern with female 'deviance' is also a major alarm for the journalists who commented on the English case. The adjectives favoured for expressing such non-passive behaviour include: 'berserk', 'Jekyll and Hydes', 'hysterical', 'a raging animal', etc.

2 A quotation from the wife of Christine English's lover, *Daily Mail*, 11 November 1981.
3 See postscript.
4 Christine English's defence counsel, *Guardian*, 11 November 1981.

References

Katharina Dalton, *Once a Month* (Fontana, London 1978).
Michel Foucault, *The History of Sexuality* (Pelican, Harmondworth 1981.

4 The selling of premenstrual syndrome:
who profits from making PMS 'the disease of the 1980s?

Andrea Eagan*

In the summer of 1961, I was working as a laboratory assistant at a major pharmaceutical firm. Seminars were regularly given on recent scientific developments, and that summer, one of them, on the oral contraceptive, was given by an associate of Dr Gregory Pincus, who was instrumental in the development of the Pill. As a rule, only the scientists went to the seminars. But for this one, every woman in the place - receptionists and bottle washers, technicians and cleaners - showed up. Oral contraception sounded like a miracle, a dream come true.

During the discussion, someone asked whether the drug was safe. Yes, we were assured, it was perfectly safe. It had been thoroughly tested in Puerto Rico, and besides, you were only adjusting the proportions of naturally occurring substances in the body, putting in a little estrogen and progesterone to fool the body into thinking that it was 'just a little bit pregnant'. The Food and Drug Administration had approved the sale of the birth-control pill in the United States the year before. News of it was everywhere. Women flocked to their doctors to get it. The dream, we now know, was much too good to be true. But we learned that only after years of using the Pill, after we had already become a generation of guinea pigs.

Since then, and because of similar experiences with DES and with estrogen replacement therapy (ERT), because of the work of the women's health movement and of health activists like Barbara

---

* Andrea Boroff Eagan is a health activist and president of the National Writers' Union This article first appeared in *Ms*, October 1983.

Seaman, we have presumably learned something: we have become cautious about medical miracles and scientific breakthroughs. To suddenly discover, then, that thousands of women are rushing to get an untested drug to cure a suspected but entirely unproved hormone deficiency which manifests itself as a condition with a startling variety of symptoms – known by the catchall name premenstrual syndrome (PMS) – is a little shocking.

Often when a drug suddenly makes the news, or when a new 'disease', for which there is a patented cure is discovered, it is fairly easy to find the public relations work of the drug manufacturers behind the story. As just one example, estrogen replacement therapy for the symptoms of the menopause had been around since the 1940s. But in 1966, a Brooklyn physician by the name of Robert Wilson wrote a book called *Feminine Forever*, which extolled the benefits of ERT in preventing what the author called 'living decay'. Wilson went on TV and radio, was interviewed for scores of articles. He claimed that *lifelong* ERT, starting well before menopause, would prevent or cure more than twenty different conditions, ranging from backaches to insomnia and irritability. Wilson ran an operation called the Wilson Research Foundation that put out information to the media and received grants from drug companies. Among those contributing to the Wilson Foundation was Ayerst Laboratories, the largest manufacturer of the estrogen used in the treatment of menopause symptoms. Ayerst also funded a group called the Information Center on the Mature Woman, from which regular information bulletins were sent to the media.

Many doctors had misgivings about ERT (the link between estrogen and cancer had been reported since the 1930s), but the information that the public received about ERT was almost entirely positive. One of the few warnings against ERT appeared in *Ms* in December 1972. Three years later, in 1975, a study was published in the *New England Journal of Medicine* reporting that estrogen users had a five to fourteen times greater incidence of uterine cancer than did non-users. This *was* news, and it made the papers. (The *New England Journal*, like several other prestigious medical journals, sends out advance issues to some news services, which is why the networks all have the same story on the same day.)

Women, needless to say, were concerned about ERT. Many simply stopped taking the drug, and sales of Premarin (the brand name of Ayerst's ERT preparation, which accounted for 80 per cent of the market) dropped.

Soon after this, Ayerst received a memo on media strategy from Hill & Knowlton, its public relations firm. This memo, the sort that is supposed to be absolutely confidential, became public when someone sent a copy to the New York women's newspaper, *Majority Report*. *MR* published the entire memo under the headline 'New Discovery: Public Relations Cures Cancer'. The first part of the plan was to take the spotlight off estrogen and refocus it on menopause. The 'estrogen message', said the memo, 'can be effectively conveyed by discreet references to products that your doctor may prescribe'. Articles on menopause were to be placed in major women's magazines. Information was also to be fed to syndicated women's page columnists, general magazines, and prominent science writers and editors.

The second part of Hill & Knowlton's plan was to counter anticipated negative publicity. A list of potentially damaging events – research reports (one was expected from the Mayo Clinic), FDA announcements, lawsuits – was given. News releases were to be prepared *in advance* of the 'damaging commentary . . . in as much detail as possible'. When this memo became public (Jack Anderson picked it up after *MR*'s publication), Ayerst denied any intention of following its recommendations, but the memo actually outlines the kinds of steps some drug manufacturers take to bring their products to the attention of the public and to counteract criticism.

The same story, with only minor changes, can be told for a number of other drugs, so when I began seeing articles about PMS and progesterone treatment, I immediately had some questions. Why was PMS suddenly 'news'? What do we really know about progesterone? And who are the advocates of this treatment?

PMS stories began appearing rather suddenly about two years ago, after two Englishwomen claimed PMS as a mitigating factor in their defence against murder charges. When the stories about these cases appeared, many American women who suffer from cyclical problems naturally became interested in finding out all they could about the condition.

PMS itself is not news. It was first mentioned in the medical literature in the 1930s, and women presumably had it before then.

Estimates on the numbers of women affected by PMS vary wildly. Some claim that as many as 80 per cent are affected while others place estimates at only 20 per cent. Similarly, doctor's opinions vary on the number and type of symptoms that may indicate PMS. They cite from 20 up to 150 physical and psychological symptoms, ranging from bloating to rage. The key to recognizing PMS and differentiating it from anything else that might cause some or all of a woman's symptoms is timing. The symptoms appear at some point after ovulation (around mid-cycle) and disappear at the beginning of the menstrual period. (It should not be confused with dysmenorrhea or menstrual discomfort, about which much is known, and for which several effective safe treatments have been developed.)

While PMS is now generally acknowledged to be a physical, as well as a psychological disorder, there is little agreement on what causes it or how it should be treated. There are at least half a dozen theories as to its cause – ranging from an alteration in the way that the body uses glucose, to excessive estrogen levels – none of which have been convincingly demonstrated.

One of the most vocal proponents of PMS treatment is Katharina Dalton, a British physician who has been treating the condition for more than thirty years. Dalton believes that PMS results from a deficiency of progesterone, a hormone that is normally present at high levels during the seocnd half of the menstrual cycle and during pregnancy. Her treatment, and that of her followers, relies on the administration of progesterone during the premenstrual phase of the cycle.

Progesterone is not absorbed effectively when taken by mouth. Powdered progesterone, derived from yams or soybeans, can be dissolved in oil and given in deep, painful muscular injections. Or the powder can be absorbed from vaginal or rectal suppositories, a more popular form. (In this country the Upjohn Company is the major manufacturer of progesterone, which they sell only in bulk to pharmacies where pharmacists then package it for sale. Upjohn makes no recommendation for the use of progesterone and is conducting no tests on the product.)

Although she promotes the progesterone treatment, Dalton has no direct evidence of a hormone deficiency in PMS sufferers. Because progesterone is secreted cyclically in irregular bursts, and testing of blood levels of progesterone is complicated and expensive, studies have been unable to show conclusively that women with PMS symptoms have lower levels of progesterone than other women. Dalton's evidence is indirect: the symptoms of PMS are relieved by the administration of progesterone.

Upon learning about Dalton's diagnosis-and-cure, many women concluded that they had the symptoms she was talking about. But when they asked their doctors for progesterone treatment, they generally got nowhere. Progesterone is not approved by the FDA for treatment of PMS (the only approved uses are for treating cessation of menstrual flow and abnormal uterine bleeding due to hormone imbalance); there is *nothing* in the medical literature showing clearly what causes PMS, and there has never been a well-designed, controlled study here or in England of the effect of progesterone on PMS.

Despite some doctors' reluctance to prescribe progesterone, self-help groups began springing up, and special clincs were established to treat PMS. Women who had any of the reported symptoms (cyclical or not) headed en masse for the clinics or flew thousands of miles to doctors whose willingness to prescribe progesterone had become known through the PMS network. And a few pharmacists began putting up progesterone powder in suppository form and doing a thriving business.

How did PMS suddenly become the rage, or what one New York gynaecologist called 'the hypoglycemia of the 1980s'? At least part of the publicity can be traced to an enterprising young man called James Hovey. He is reported to have claimed he had a BA in public health from UCLA despite the fact that, aside from extension courses, he had been there less than a year. (UCLA does not even have a BA programme in public health.) He met Katharina Dalton in Holland several years ago at a conference on the biological basis of violent behaviour. Returning to the United States, he worked with a Boston physician who opened the first PMS clinic in Lynnfield. A few months later, Hovey left the clinic. He then started The National Center for Premenstrual Syndrome and Menstrual Distress in New York City, Boston, Memphis and Los Angeles – each with a local doctor as medical director.

For $265 (paid in advance), you got three visits. The initial visit consisted of a physical exam and interview, and a lengthy questionnaire on symptoms. During the second visit, the clinic dispensed advice on diet and vitamins, and reviewed a monthly record the patient was asked to keep. On the third visit, if symptoms still persisted, most patients received a prescription for progesterone.

Last year, James Hovey's wife Donna, a nurse who was working in his New York clinic, told me that they were participating in an FDA-approved study of progesterone, in conjunction with a doctor from the University of Tennessee. In fact, to date the FDA has approved only one study on progesterone treatment of PMS, which is conducted at the National Institute of Child Health and Human Development, an organization unrelated to James Hovey.

Similar contradictions and misrepresentations, as well as Hovey's lack of qualifications to be conducting research or running a medical facility, were exposed by two journalists last year. Marilyn Webb in the *Village Voice* and Jennifer Allen in *New York* magazine both dug into the operation of the clinic and Hovey's past to reveal him as a former Army medical corpsman turned entrepreneur. Hovey left New York and gave up his interest in the New York and Boston clinics. He is currently running a nationwide PMS referral service out of New Hampshire.

In a recent interview, Hovey said that the clinic business is too time-consuming, and that he is getting out. His 'only interest is research' he said. He was associated with two scientists who applied to the FDA for permission to do progesterone studies but who were rejected because the FDA considered the doses of progesterone to be too high. At last report, Hovey still headed H and K Pharmaceuticals, a company founded in 1981 for the manufacture of progesterone suppositories, and it is as a supplier that his name has appeared on FDA applications.

Hovey's involvement in PMS treatment seems to have centred on the commercial opportunities. Others, such as Virginia Cassara, became interested in PMS for more personal reasons.

Cassara, a social worker from Wisconsin, went to England in 1979 to be treated by Dalton for severe PMS. The treatment was successful and Cassara returned to spread the good news. She invited Katharina Dalton to Wisconsin to speak and notified the press. Though only one article appeared, it brought women 'out of the closet', Cassara says. Cassara began counselling and speaking, selling Dalton's books and other literature. Her national group, PMS Action, now has an annual budget of $650,000, 17 paid staff members, and 40 volunteers. Cassara spends most of her time travelling and speaking.

Cassara's argument is compelling, at least initially. She describes the misery of PMS sufferers, and the variety of ineffective medical treatments they have been subjected to in their search for relief. For anyone who is sensitive to women's health issues, it is a familiar tale: a condition that afflicts perhaps millions of women has never been studied; a treatment that gives relief is ignored. Women, says Cassara, are pushed into diet and exercise regimens that are difficult to maintain and don't always work. One valid solution, she feels, lies in progesterone.

According to FDA spokesperson Roger Eastep, Phase I studies – those that determine how much a particular substance is absorbed by the body and how it works – have yet to be done for progesterone. But in the meantime, more and more doctors are prescribing the hormone for PMS.

Dr Michelle Harrison, a gynaecologist practising in Cambridge, Massachusetts, and a spokesperson for the National Women's Health Network, is one physician who does prescribe progesterone to some women with mixed feelings. 'I've seen it dramatically temper women's reactions', she says. 'For those women whose lives are shattered by PMS, who've made repeated suicide attempts or who are unable to keep a job, you have to do something. But I have a very frightening consent form that they have to sign before I'll give progesterone to them.' Harrison also stresses that a lot of PMS is iatrogenic; that is, it is caused by medical treatment. It often appears for the first time after a woman has stopped taking birth-control pills, after tubal ligation or even after a hysterectomy, in which the ovaries have been removed.

When doctors do prescribe progesterone, their ideas of the appropriate dosage can vary from 50 to 2400 mg per day. For some women, dosages at the lower end of the scale do not bring relief from their symptoms. It has also been reported by women taking progesterone and in medical literature that the effect of a particular dose diminishes after a few months. Some women are symptom-free as long as they are taking the drug, but the symptoms reappear as soon as they stop, regardless of where they are in the menstrual cycle.

For all these reasons, some women are taking much higher doses than their doctors prescribe. Michelle Harrison had heard of women taking 2400 mg per day; Dalton had heard about 3000; Cassara knows women who take 4000. Because PMS symptoms tend to occur when progesterone is not being taken, some women take it every day, instead of only during the premenstrual phase. Some bleed all the time; others don't menstruate at all. Vaginal and rectal swelling are common. Animal studies have shown increased rates of breast tumours and cervical cancer. Marilyn Webb, a reporter who began taking progesterone while working on a story about PMS, developed chest pains after several months. She asked all the doctors she interviewed whether any of their patients had experienced chest pains. Every one said that she or he had at least one patient who had.

Reminding her of the history of the Pill, of DES and of ERT, I asked Virginia Cassara whether she was concerned about the long-term effects of progesterone on women. 'I guess I don't think there could be anything worse than serious PMS', she responded. 'Even cancer?' I asked. 'Absolutely. Even cancer.' Later she said, 'I think it's paternalistic of the FDA to make those choices for us, to tell us what we can and cannot put in our bodies. Women with PMS are competent beings, capable of making their own choices.'

I don't have severe PMS, and I don't think I fully understand the desperation of women who do and who see help at last within reach. But given our limited understanding of how progesterone works, I

do not understand why women like Cassara are echoing drug company complaints of overregulation by the FDA. I'm alarmed to see women flocking to use an untested substance about which there is substantial suspicion, whose mode of action is not known, to treat a condition whose very cause is a mystery. And I fear that, somewhere down the line, we will finally learn all about progesterone treatment and it won't be what we wanted to know.

One doctor, who refused to be quoted by name, cheerfully assured me that progesterone was safe. 'Even if a woman is taking 1600 milligrams per day, the amount of circulating progesterone is still only a quarter of what is normally circulating during pregnancy.' And I couldn't help but think of the doctor at the seminar more than twenty years ago: 'Of course it's safe. It's just like being a little bit pregnant.'

Postscript

The vitamin cure

Diet and vitamin therapies are, according to many doctors, effective in the large majority of PMS cases. Michelle Harrison has found that most of her patients will respond to a hypoglycemia diet: whole grains, no caffeine, lots of water, no sugar, frequent small meals. To this, she adds up to 800 mg per day of vitamin B_6 during the premenstrual phase. Harrison has written a clear and useful 50-page booklet, *Self-Help for Premenstrual Syndrome* ($4.50, plus $1.50 postage and handling from Matrix Press, Box 740M, Cambridge, Massachusetts 02238), which includes charts for keeping track of symptoms and lots of good advice about diagnosis and treatment, as well as a look at the social and political questions raised by PMS.

Dr Marcia Storch (author of *How to Relieve Cramps and Other Menstrual Problems*, Workman Publishing, $3.95) and her associate Dr Shelley Kolton, believe that reducing salt intake helps to curb water retention and headaches that result from it. They also prescribe 300 to 500 mg daily of vitamin B_6. Kolton says that this therapy is effective in about 80 per cent of all cases, though it may take several months for the treatment to work. (Storch and Kolton do not recommend progesterone because of safety concerns.) (A.E.)

Dr Dalton's cure
As early as 1948, Dr Katharina Dalton recognized and treated PMS. Trained as a podiatrist, she later went to medical school and shifted her practice to PMS treatment after her own premenstrual headaches were relieved by monthly doses of progesterone.

'I've seen no ill effects in the thirty years I've used it', Dalton says. 'The women with severe PMS deserve treatment.'

Dalton agrees that eating starches and refraining from the use of birth-control pills does help alleviate PMS. But she questions the value of some alternative approaches. 'There is much emphasis on these mighty vitamins. And exercise, which *is* conducive to good health. But it is irrelevant, except that it improves a patient's outlook.'

While many researchers credit Dalton with drawing attention to the complaints linked to some women's menstrual cycles, they worry about the application of her ideas. 'Dalton shows a pretty scary view of women who have PMS', says Dr Estelle Ramey, a physiology professor at Georgetown University. 'I'm afraid we could be digging a grave for women leaders.'

Dalton, however, disagrees: 'I come from a country where we have a female monarch and a female prime minister. We can't deny our biology. We've got to help women who are suffering.' (Lavinia Edmunds)

References

Donald C. Smith, Ross Prentice, Donovan J. Thompson and Walter L. Herrmann, 'Association of Exogenous Estrogen and Endometrical Carcinoma', *The New England Journal of Medicine*, **293**, no. 23 (4 December 1975), pp. 1164–7.

Robert A. Wilson, *Feminine Forever* (M. Evans and Company, New York 1966).

Appendix
Women's Health Information Centre

The Women's Health Information Centre is a national information and resource centre for women's health issues. Since we received our first grant two years ago we have built up a library of pamphlets, books, journal articles, videos, tapes and posters. We have an ever-growing national register of women's health groups, self-help groups, well-woman campaigns and voluntary organizations.

We answer inquiries by photocopying relevant papers from the library, recommending books, lending videos, and giving addresses of support groups and voluntary organizations. We have a few of our own publications to sell, and others we have ordered to sell that are difficult to obtain. We are not an advice centre for clinical problems, nor a referral agency to medical or alternative practitioners.

WHIC is open to women who want to use the library on Tuesdays and Thursdays from 10 to 4 o'clock.

For further information:

WHIC
52 Featherstone Street
London EC1
Telephone 01-251 6580/6589

Subscribe to the WHIC newsletter: £5 for groups or individuals, £1.50 unwaged.